D1072352

PETAWAWA
PUBLIC LIBRARY

The Smythe Family, the Gardens and the

CENTRE

Toronto Maple Leafs Hockey Club

ICE

The Smythe Family, the Gardens and the

CENTRE

Toronto Maple Leafs Hockey Club

ICE

Thomas Stafford Smythe

with

Kevin Shea

foreword by

Wayne Gretzky

Fenn Publishing Company Limited

Bolton Canada

CENTRE ICE
A Fenn Publishing Book / October 2000

Interior design: McGraphics Desktop Publishing
Jacket design: Kathryn Del Borrello
Editorial : Laura Pratt
Publisher: C. Jordan Fenn

Fenn Publishing Company Ltd.
Bolton, Ontario, Canada

Distributed in Canada by H. B. Fenn and Company Ltd.
34 Nixon Road, Bolton, Ontario, Canada, L7E 1W2

visit us on the World Wide Web, at www.hbfenn.com

Canadian Cataloguing in Publication Data

Smythe, Thomas Stafford
Centre Ice: the Smythe family, the Gardens and the Toronto Maple Leafs Hockey Club

Includes index
ISBN 1-55168-250-8

1. Smythe, Thomas Stafford. 2. Smythe, Thomas Stafford — Family.
3. Toronto Maple Leafs (Hockey team). 4. Maple Leaf Gardens Ltd.
5. National Hockey League. I. Shea, Kevin, 1956- . II. Title

GV848.5S592A3 2000 796.962'092 C00-931985-9

Printed and bound in Canada

In Loving Memory of my Dear Friend and Sister
Victoria (Vicky) Rose
1942–2000

Contents

NHL President, John Ziegler, presenting the *Conn Smythe Trophy* to Edmonton captain, Wayne Gretzky, following his 43 points — 12 goals and 31 assists — in the Oiler's 1988 Stanley Cup victory over the Boston Bruins.

The Conn Smythe Trophy is an annual award presented to the most valuable player for his team in the playoffs. The winner is selected by the Professional Hockey Writers' Association at the conclusion of the final game in the Stanley Cup finals.

Maple Leaf Gardens Limited first presented the Conn Smythe Trophy in 1965 to Montreal Canadien, John Beliveau, to honor Conn Smythe, the former coach, manager, president and owner-governor of the Toronto Maple Leafs.

Foreword by Wayne Gretzky

If ever I had wondered exactly what Maple Leaf Gardens meant to Canadians, I found my answer almost by accident last February when the National Hockey League held its 50th All-Star Game in Toronto. The actual game, of course, was held at the fabulous new Air Canada Centre, but I had made private arrangements to have just one more skate at the Gardens that Saturday morning. We didn't tell a soul about the plans apart from a few very close friends who I knew would like nothing better than to join me for a skate on the very same ice surface that all their great heroes — players from King Clancy to Dave Keon and Darryl Sittler — had played on. I figured we'd skate, play a little shinny, and take a few photographs to mark the occasion. But the one thing I never expected was that half the people on the ice would be carrying cell phones, and they'd be calling friends all over the country just to let them know where they were and what they were doing — even if it meant waking relatives still sound asleep out in Alberta and British Columbia.

I could well understand the sentiment. Maple Leaf Gardens was my Augusta National, my Yankee Stadium, the one place on earth where hockey — my game — most deserved to be played. It was where I saw my very first NHL game when I was

six years old. I went with my grandmother, who was a lifelong Leafs fan, and we had seats in the very last row of the greys. The Leafs were playing the Oakland Seals. Worst seat in the house and probably the worst team in the league — but I felt like I was in heaven. I even remember teasing my grandmother that one day I'd be playing here. Only I'd be with the Detroit Red Wings, my team back then because Gordie Howe played for the Wings, and we'd be beating her beloved Leafs and her favourite Leafs player, Frank Mahovlich. I never did play for the Wings, and never did get to play against the Big M, but I can't say my dream didn't come true. I got to play in the Gardens, after all.

I laugh sometimes when I read about ticket prices and how much they've gone up. There was a time when a kid could get into the Gardens for a buck — so long as he was in the Marlboros organization and could prove it by his jacket. When I was fourteen and left Brantford to play in Toronto for the Young Nationals, I was lucky enough to board with a family whose older son had once played for the Marlies, and I used to borrow his old hockey jacket, jump on the subway, and get there in time to watch the warm-ups. It was wonderful. For a buck I got to stand there and watch the greatest players in the world do the most amazing things with pucks. That's when I first started dreaming seriously about one day being in this same league, playing in this very same building.

I never got to meet the man who built that extraordinary hockey shrine, but I did happily become good friends with Conn Smythe's grandson, Tom, whom I first met, rather appropriately, at one of the first Conn Smythe dinners. For me, it would be the first of many, for it's difficult to imagine a better evening or a better cause. I guess I must have been about seventeen years old at that first one, and I remember going because they were going to honour Guy Lafleur that night and I was a huge fan of the Flower. I got to meet him and it was great, but I also got to meet a lot of other marvellous people that night, and one of them was Tom, who quickly became a lifelong friend.

Tom shares a very special name in our game. Conn Smythe, probably more than anyone else, is responsible for making the National Hockey League the strong and dynamic force it is today. It was largely his vision that made hockey one of the major North American sports and, most obviously, his vision that built Maple Leaf Gardens back in 1931 and made hockey rinks — large, bright, awe-inspiring rinks — a significant part of the NHL experience.

In 1985, the year the Edmonton Oilers beat the Philadelphia Flyers for their second straight Stanley Cup, I was fortunate enough to be awarded the Conn Smythe Trophy as the playoffs Most Valuable Player. I remember the moment they announced it turning to Paul Coffey, who'd had a great series, and telling him, "It could just as easily have been you." Three years later, when we took Boston in five games, I was lucky enough to win it again. And I use that word "lucky" deliberately — the Conn Smythe is such a hard, hard trophy to win you need a certain amount of luck. First, you've got to stay healthy over four rounds, and that's no simple task in Stanley Cup play. Then, your team pretty much has to take the Cup itself, because apart from very few exceptions — usually goaltenders — the Conn Smythe goes to a member of the successful team.

Winning the Stanley Cup is, any hockey player will tell you, the greatest experience anyone can possibly have in the game, but let me assure you that the Smythe is second best. The presentation is done right there on the ice, which makes an event of it and also makes everyone on the team feel a part of it. They might hand it out as an individual trophy, but everyone who has ever won the Conn Smythe would tell you that it is truly a team trophy, and the ultimate compliment a team can offer one of its players. The Conn Smythe Trophy, like the Stanley Cup itself, is unique, and a treasure for the game of hockey.

CENTRE ICE

I never had the privilege of playing for the Stanley Cup in Maple Leaf Gardens, but I did get a sense of it in the spring of 1993 when the Los Angeles Kings played that amazing semi-final against the Leafs. The place was absolutely electric to be in that spring and there was never any question that the series could have gone either way at almost every time. I was fortunate to get a hat trick that seventh game and it was us, not the Leafs, that moved on to play Montreal in the final. We couldn't quite do the job and I don't know if the Leafs would have fared that much better against Patrick Roy and the Canadiens, but I do know for sure that a Toronto-Montreal final, with games in the old Forum and the old Gardens, would have been one of the highlights of the NHL's first century.

Anyone who has ever been to the Gardens, anyone who has ever played in the Gardens, knows that it was a special, magical experience. It's sad that the Gardens no longer plays host to NHL games, but, to me, it is a marvel that the new Air Canada Centre has managed to recreate much of that magic. I don't know how they did it, but there is something about the lighting, the ice, the crackle in the air, that feels like Maple Leaf Gardens the moment you enter the ACC to see a Leafs game.

In some ways, that makes the end of the Gardens a little easier to accept. You don't replace a shrine like the Gardens, you cannot replicate the Stanley Cups won or the heroics fans saw in that building, but you can honour the memory of the building by carrying that special atmosphere into the new rink — and somehow they have managed to this.

The Air Canada Centre is a splendid facility, perhaps the best modern rink in the game, and while I'm a little bit disappointed not to be able to say I played in this marvellous new rink, there's a part of me that is both proud and content that my Toronto games took place in real life where they always had in my dreams: Maple Leaf Gardens. In both memory and hockey history, it will stand forever.

Wayne Gretzky

Introduction by Dick Duff

At the closing of Maple Leaf Gardens, Tommy Smythe and I renewed our friendship. He informed me he was writing a book about the Gardens and especially his grandfather, Major Conn Smythe. I offered my congratulations and support and enclose some thoughts.

During my early days with the Leafs, Tom was the stickboy for Saturday night games. Being around the team, he picked up on what it meant for us to be part of Canada's team. The respect we had for its traditions, the Gardens itself and all who worked there.

Tommy later became active and successful in the Marlboros organization. Some of the greatest Leaf players had their start with the Toronto Marlboros. In a way, Tom's future role as General Manger and President of the Toronto Maple Leafs was being prepared. We now know that this didn't happen. Tom's book deals with the Smythe's family loss of the Leafs and the Gardens.

I respect Tommy Smythe. He has endured a serious illness that many tough and courageous athletes would have trouble dealing with. I wish him always the best. I was a proud Leaf and though Major Conn Smythe was demanding, he built a great hockey franchise that Canadians will always feel is part of the their culture.

Tommy, our first Stanley Cup party at your home, with your father Stafford, grandfather Conn and gentleman Joe Primeau remains one of my most treasured times.

Dick Duff

Chapter One

The Smythe Legacy

Ted Kennedy, the captain of the Toronto Maple Leafs, skated over to the bench and stopped just in front of the open gate with a spray of ice shavings. He leaned over the boards near where I was standing and said, "Hey Tommy, get me another stick — I cracked my blade." Without so much as a nod, I hustled over to the rack of spare sticks in the hallway outside the Leafs dressing room and grabbed a new one. I barely had to glance at the #9 written up on the shaft near the tape knob to know it was Ted's. Each player's stick had unique differences, which were easily visible to me. Hurrying back, I handed him the new stick. He had already given his cracked one to Bob Haggert, the Maple Leafs' assistant trainer. Kennedy grabbed the stick from me, leaned down on it hard to test the flexibility, then gave me a little wink and skated back to the face-off circle. I took immense pride in the fact that I had done my job well, and that "Teeder," one of the Maple Leafs' favourite players, had shown me a little extra attention. After all, how many six-year-olds have such a bird's eye view of Canada's favourite hockey team?

I came to realize that I did indeed have a very special vantage point from which I was able to watch the proceedings of the Toronto Maple Leafs hockey team and Maple Leaf Gardens over the course of five decades. My name is Tom Smythe. My family name is the one most closely aligned with the history of the Toronto Maple Leaf franchise. And my family presided over the Toronto Maple Leafs for every single one of the team's 11 Stanley Cup victories. My dad, Stafford, was president of the Toronto Maple Leafs and Maple Leaf Gardens during the 1960s, a decade that included the Leafs' last four Stanley Cup victories. And my grandfather, Conn Smythe, built Maple Leaf Gardens and ran the Leaf operation from the late 1920s through to the beginning of the '60s, winning seven Stanley Cups during that time.

I can truthfully say I grew up in Maple Leaf Gardens. From the time I was born, I was in and around hockey. My grandfather always had a vision that the Toronto Maple Leaf organization and Maple Leaf Gardens would be a Smythe family dynasty. Conn Smythe would run the team until he felt his son Stafford was ready to take over the operation then my grandfather would sell majority ownership to him. Dad would oversee Maple Leaf Gardens and the Leafs until he felt I was ready to take over, then turn the organization over to me. Sadly, the plan took a twist no one anticipated and I never got the opportunity to continue the Smythe tradition at Maple Leaf Gardens into a third generation.

From the perspective of a six-year-old, there was no greater way to spend a Saturday night than standing behind the bench of the Toronto Maple Leafs. I realized early that there was a destiny laid out in front of me, and I worked very hard to earn the trust I would need to fulfill this promise. I went from stickboy to scout, later moving into the executive ranks of the Toronto Marlboros Junior A hockey team, first as assistant general manager, later as general manager. With each progressive step, I soaked up every bit of knowledge I could.

The path prepared for me was never smooth. Both my grandfather, Conn, and my father, Stafford, made certain I took nothing for granted. Grandpa and Dad wanted me to earn everything I was ever given, and believe me, I did. During my initial two years of high school at Upper Canada College, an illustrious all-boys private school in Toronto, my alarm went off at 3:30 each morning. I was picked up at 4am and taken to Woodbine Racetrack, where I worked in my grandfather's stable exercising his two-year-old horses. A car dropped me off at school for 9:00. I had a full day of studying, then at 3:30 in the afternoon, all students had to participate in some form of physical activity. For me, it was usually gymnastics — I loved the parallel bars and the exhilaration provided by the trampoline. A quick shower at 5:00pm, and then it was off scouting hockey players somewhere in southern Ontario with some of the scouting staff of the Toronto Maple Leafs and their junior hockey affiliate, the Toronto Marlboros. When the final buzzer of that game rang, the scouting party hunted for a meal. My head never hit the pillow before one in the morning, only to be jolted awake once again in a few hour's time. I don't know how I did it, but I know why: it was the price I had to pay to gain access to the world in which I wanted to live: the world of running the Toronto Maple Leafs and Maple Leaf Gardens.

There are a million stories within the walls of Maple Leaf Gardens and the Smythe family. Some have been chronicled in the numerous books, magazines and newspaper articles published over the past few decades. But many other stories have never seen the light of day, and those tales deserve to be told. I was given the unique opportunity of seeing the operation in a way that only a few others ever did. I participated in many of the franchise's most celebrated moments, and lived through some of its very darkest times as well. No one can imagine the great fun it was spending time at Maple Leaf Gardens and growing up a part of the Leaf family. Yet, there were things I saw that I never should have seen. There were things I heard that I never should have heard. And there were things I experienced that I wish I never had. It was a privilege to share travel, meals and ideas with some of the brightest minds in hockey history. It was a thrill to look out over the ice and watch some of the greatest players ever to lace up a pair of skates. From an enthusiastic young man's perspective, I couldn't have been more involved in the Toronto Maple Leafs organization if I had been the one taking faceoffs at centre ice.

Chapter Two

Father and Son

When World War II broke out, both my grandfather and father enlisted for active service. For Conn, it was no easy accomplishment, as he was 44 years old and had already served with distinction in World War I. In fact, Grandpa had received the Military Cross for being wounded during the first World War, later spending time in a Polish prison camp. But with the outbreak of World War II, my grandfather insisted on being sent to Europe by exerting pressure on the enlistment board. He formed a Sportsmen's Battalion and after continual urging, was finally cleared for active duty. My Dad, meanwhile, signed up for the Navy.

Although Stafford and Conn were very close most of their lives, there was definitely a competitive energy between the two that often resulted in friction. While Conn's other children, Miriam and Hugh, had the sweet disposition of my grandmother Irene, Stafford was much more like his father. Grandpa had a strong, forceful personality that he liked to impose on those around him. As the general manager of a hockey team or the president of a company — or better yet, as an officer in the army — this kind of person makes for a strong and capable leader. But when that discipline is applied to a father — son relationship, there are bound to be sparks.

Conn would push my Dad, trying to make him stronger; in his opinion, trying to make him a better man. Early on in Stafford's life, my grandfather questioned Dad's choices. Grandpa felt that Dad was too easily swayed and unfocused and that he often made poor judgement calls on his choice of acquaintances. While Miriam and Hugh played contentedly with their friends, Stafford ran with a tougher crowd of boys and was constantly in trouble. Although Dad respected Conn for his accomplishments, he balked at his domineering attitude, and often rebelled by trying to distance himself from Grandpa's authoritarian stance.

I am certain that Dad felt compelled to enlist in the Canadian war effort of his own accord, but purposely stayed away from the Army where his father was an officer. Instead, Dad joined the Royal Canadian Navy in 1940, and rose within the ranks to become a lieutenant.

Throughout their lives, Conn and Stafford competed in everything they did. From the time he was a young boy, Stafford caddied for Conn during golf games. As Dad grew up to play the game himself, he and Grandpa would often play, yet Dad never won. Never. Grandpa was an ardent and aggressive golfer and extremely talented at applying his intelligence to winning games. When the two would play, Stafford would grit his teeth through 18 holes, lose and come home in a rage. After the Leafs won the Stanley Cup in 1963, the Smythe families vacationed in Palm Beach, Florida. By this time, Conn was in his late sixties, Dad was in his forties and I was in my teens. I remember my father and I were sitting in the kitchen of our Florida home one morning when he sat bolt upright, sparked with an idea. "Tommy, call up your granddad and set up a golf game for he and I." Amazed, I replied, "sure Dad, but why go through the hassle? You know Grandpa beats you every time. Then you come home angry and we can't talk to you for hours." Stafford didn't seem concerned one bit. "Just call him, Tommy. I think I know a way that I can beat him this time."

Grandpa agreed to the challenge, and with a sly chuckle, told me, "Fine Tommy. Tell your Dad he's on, and that I'm going to whip him like I've done every single time before." My father and I drove over to the challenging course and waited for Conn. "Okay Tommy, I need you to caddy for me," Dad began. "But more importantly, whenever I sink my putt, just leave the ball in the hole. You got me?"

"But Dad, I stammered, "What am I going to do that for?" Dad smiled. "Trust me, Tom, just trust me."

Conn had a terrible habit of playing out of turn. In every game he played, he'd drive the ball down the fairway, then rather than wait his turn, he'd continue to play the ball until he had sunk it in the cup. It frustrated his opponents and threw them into distraction. But this time, it was Stafford who played his own mind game. On the first hole, Dad drove the ball beautifully down the fairway. Conn responded in kind. The two played onto the green. Conn sunk his putt on his fourth stroke. Stafford shot a five, but once he had put the ball in the cup, I returned the flag to the hole and Dad and I walked off the green. "Hey!" Conn yelled. "Didn't you forget something?" Dad calmly said, "No," and walked away.

By the fourth or fifth hole, Conn was steaming. "Why the hell are you leaving your goddamn ball in the cup, Stafford?" "Dad," said Stafford calmly, "the damn things are only worth about 89 cents. Who cares?" Hole after hole, the drama continued.

After the 18th hole, Stafford had won by three strokes. Grandpa, Dad and I walked back to the parking lot. My grandfather was beet red, clenching his teeth near rage. Stafford extended his hand. "It was a pleasure to beat you for the first time ever," my father said snidely. Conn just turned away.

My Dad asked me to drive his Cadillac convertible home. We were heading down the road, when Stafford climbed clumsily into the backseat. As I looked in the rearview mirror, I saw Dad tossing his golf bag, clubs and all onto the shoulder of the road.

"Keep driving, Tommy," Dad said. "Now that I've beaten your grandfather, I'm never playing golf again." And he didn't.

"How did you know that you could distract Grandpa and throw him off his game?" I asked, incredulous. "Well Tom, it goes back to a story that just popped into my head this morning. Years ago, Conn used to play golf with R.A. Laidlaw, one of the original board members of Maple Leaf Gardens. He owned a lumber company at the time, although he's got a trucking firm now. When he and your grandfather would golf, Laidlaw would tie his tee to a string attached to his belt loop. It made your Grandpa nuts. R.A. Laidlaw would tee off, then reel in the little wooden tee and tuck it in his pocket. Conn finally exploded one day. "Laidlaw," he hollered. "You own a successful lumber company, and yet you keep the goddamned 2-cent tee after every drive like it was gold-plated or something." Mr. Laidlaw would just smile and continue to play, but it irritated your grandfather so badly that it threw him off his game and he couldn't win. That's the lesson I remembered. Utilize your brain and you can win unimaginable battles small and large. Throw someone off their game son, and they just can't function rationally."

My father applied this knowledge throughout much of his career in hockey. In a sports arena, it's dramatically easier to win, when an opponent's focus is distracted from their game.

Chapter Three

Returning Home

There had been talk of putting the National Hockey League on hold for the duration of WWII, but that idea had been averted. The National Hockey League Governors felt that the entertainment provided by professional hockey was, in itself, a morale booster for North Americans during one of this continent's darkest times. The Brooklyn Americans, renamed from the New York Americans for the 1941-42 season in order to help local attendance, suspended their operation at the beginning of the 1942-43 hockey season, a move that became permanent. As a result, the NHL in 1942-43 was comprised of the Boston Bruins, the Chicago Blackhawks, the Detroit Red Wings, the New York Rangers, the Montreal Canadiens and, of course, the Toronto Maple Leafs. The era of the "Original Six" was born, although misnamed because they certainly weren't the league's original franchises. The National Hockey League would remain constant with these six teams until the conclusion of the 1966-67 season-the last year the Toronto Maple Leafs won the Stanley Cup. In 1967-68, expansion would increase the NHL to 12 teams.

While Conn was away in England preparing for battle in August 1942, my Dad took leave from the naval base in Halifax where he was training, flew home to Toronto, and married

Dorothea Gaudette. Dad and Mom, who to this day we call "Dot," had dated for a number of years. What should have been a time of happiness for Mom and Dad sparked a fight within the Smythe family. Conn was furious because Mom was Roman Catholic, and he never approved of Dad seeing a girl "outside the faith." The Smythe family was Protestant. My Grandfather came from a different era, when a person's religion loomed large when it came to choosing a spouse. The religion issue made the wedding arrangements cumbersome and Stafford and Dorothea were forced to make the plans in secret. When Conn's wife Irene learned of Stafford and Dot's plans, she called Conn in a panic to let him know that their son was to be married within a few days. Conn was enraged and tried to make certain that the Protestant Church refused to conduct the ceremony. The Roman Catholic Church refused to allow my father and mother to marry in their church because Stafford was Protestant. Mom and Dad ended up having two small ceremonies — one in the vestibule of a Roman Catholic church, followed by another at St. Charles United Church on Baby Point Road in Toronto; right near the home of Conn and Irene. Both were relatively small family services, and although my grandfather opposed the marriage, he put his anger aside and attempted to be there to witness his son's union. Unfortunately Conn could not obtain a furlough allowing for his arrival in Toronto on time. Nonetheless, when Grandpa returned on a leave later that month, there was a letter waiting there from Dot. Her long, handwritten prose explained that she loved my father dearly, and he loved her, and although the pressures of religion had forced them to separate in the past, their mutual love always pulled them back together. Mom assured Conn that if she and my father were blessed with children, they would be raised in a manner in which Conn would be proud. While Dad and Grandpa were away serving in the war, Mom and my grandmother became very close. Conn eventually accepted Mom, and they grew to love each other and became great friends as well.

My father returned home from the Navy in July 1945 after serving four years of duty. His train, burdened with returning servicemen, pulled into Toronto's Union Station, and Mom was there waiting for him. I have to laugh when I do the math — I was born nine months to the hour from the time of Dad's arrival. For years, every time we'd pass Union Station, Mom and Dad would tease me about being conceived in a phone booth by the arrival ramp.

Conn and Irene had an incredible cottage on Lake Simcoe that they purchased in the thirties. When the hockey season was over, they liked to move up to their northern retreat — an hour north of Toronto — for the summer, just to get away from hockey for a few months. The rest of the family — Conn and Irene's children Stafford, Miriam and Hugh, all enjoyed visiting my Grandparents up at their summer place.

In 1936, my grandmother and grandfather had a fourth child, Patricia, when Irene was 40 and Conn 41. Both Grandma and Grandpa cherished their beautiful baby daughter, but it was Conn who had a special affinity for Patricia, and adored her as only a father can. This often crusty, hard-edged war veteran melted like butter with a single smile from his little girl. And Patrician took full advantage of her ability to wrap Conn around her chubby little fingers. Patricia loved the cottage, where she could chase the butterflies that fluttered around Lake Simcoe. Under the watchful eye of my grandparents, she enjoyed skipping through the cool, shallow waters that splashed the pebbles along the edge of the beach.

Almost immediately after Dad's return to Toronto from active duty, he and my Mother drove to the cottage, excited to see the family. Expecting a jubilant homecoming welcome, Stafford and Dorothea were instead met by a grief-stricken family. Exactly one hour before Mom and Dad arrived; Patricia had been found dead on the cottage veranda. Conn and Irene had been visiting friends in the area, while the Smythe's family aide, Jessie Watson, was watching Patricia. When Grandma and Grandpa returned, they called out to Patricia, but received no response. Irene, Conn and Jessie began a frantic search that ended just as quickly as it started. The lifeless body of Patricia, only ten years old on that hot summer day in 1945, was found lying limp on the cottage porch. Irene was devastated. Conn was inconsolable. Their little angel was gone.

Mortified by her death, Conn refused the Medical Examiner his consent to perform an autopsy. He candidly stated that she was dead and no amount of medical attention would, or could bring her back. He demanded that the family be granted permission to bury her without delay. He couldn't tolerate the thought of his little girl's body undergoing an adverse postmortem examination. The exact cause of death was never determined, but Patricia had suffered from food allergies and asthma all of her life. Whether she had eaten something she shouldn't have, or had a brain aneurysm, as evidence would suggest, we never knew. On the death certificate, the attending doctor simply wrote "natural causes."

With Patricia gone, Conn's demeanor altered significantly and he remained in an uncharacteristically reserved state until my birth the following spring. My coming into the world apparently inspired the resurgence of his composure and brought a sense of harmony back to the Smythe family. I wasn't a replacement for Patricia, but a welcomed addition, which could be associated with her.

Growing up, I always felt this association and enjoyed a truly special relationship with my grandfather. A relationship, which, I noted, differed greatly from those, shared between Conn and any of my siblings or cousins. Our closeness continually grew, as did his interest in my life. In my late teens, it occurred to me that he might have connected me with Patricia. Many years later, as I reluctantly approached the topic of her death, Conn and I spoke of this and I learned that my suspicions were true. His fatherly intuitions were renewed with my birth and he inadvertently assumed a great amount of responsibility and guidance during my childhood rearing.

There's an old saying that goes, "When one door closes, another opens," and that was my grandfather's belief. He lost Patricia that July, but I was born within the year, on April 12, 1946.

Chapter Four

Stickboy

Mom and Dad took me to my first hockey game when I was four. It was a Junior game at Maple Leaf Gardens featuring the Toronto Marlboros. Before the game started, I remember playing in the hallways with Harold Ballard's sons Bill and Bob. Ballard was a friend of the Smythe family and at the time president and general manager of the Toronto Marlboros Junior hockey team. Ballard was like a second father to me when I was a boy — he was always kind and attentive. In spite of the fact that Conn and my Dad had plans for me to take over the Leafs one day in the future, I'm certain that Harold would have loved to prepared his boys for running the team one day, too. But back then, I remember vividly that Bill and Bob were far more interested in the food, running up and down the hallways begging their Mom and Dad for another hot dog or ice cream. I was much more interested in watching the hockey game.

On Sundays, Maple Leaf Gardens would host Junior A doubleheaders, with both the Toronto Marlboros and the St. Michael's Majors playing games. Ballard's daughter Mary Elizabeth and my sister Vicky would quite often come to the Gardens for these afternoon games. Although neither was much of a hockey fan, they both enjoyed the excitement and atmosphere surrounding the building and the auspicious feeling associated with being part of the Maple Leaf family.

By the time I turned six, Dad figured I was ready to start my apprenticeship. He asked the Leafs' assistant trainer, Bob Haggert, to teach me to be the stickboy. This position was one that both my father and his brother Hugh had once held when they were young boys. Dad took me into the Maple Leafs dressing room and announced me to the players. "Gentlemen, I'd like you to meet my boy Tommy. He's your new stickboy. If you have any problems with him, you just let me know." Then, Dad led me around the room, introducing me to each player individually. I'd stick out my little hand and it would disappear in the huge palms of the players. Each one was very nice to me-some kidded that I'd better not screw up; others just smiled and welcomed me to the team.

Every Maple Leaf player prepared a spare hockey stick for each game, and these extras were kept on a rack in the hall behind the Maple Leaf bench. It was my duty to keep a close eye on the players and if one broke his stick, I was to get the replacement as fast as my little legs would allow. In watching the players, I was learning the fundamentals of my burgeoning hockey career. During my time with the Leafs scouting staff, I would discover that it was essential to follow the players, not the puck. This practise taught me to know where every player — for both teams — was at any given moment. It's a valuable lesson. In many of the accolades written about Hockey Hall of Fame inductee, Wayne Gretzky, there are highly complimentary statements on how well Wayne "sees the ice." This talent separates the better players and hockey management from the rest of the pack.

My stickboy position lasted from first grade until I entered high school. My schoolmates thought it was fantastic that one of their friends was rubbing shoulders with heroes like George Armstrong, Tim Horton and my personal favourite, Dick Duff.

Four generations of Smythe men have attended Toronto's Upper Canada College, a private boy's high school. Conn attended UCC for a couple of years before his father could no longer afford to send him there, at which time he transferred to Jarvis Collegiate. Conn later attended the University of Toronto's School of Practical Science, where he earned his engineering degree. Stafford went to UCC for a year, then attended Runnymede Collegiate. My dad also graduated with his engineering degree from the University of Toronto. I went to Upper Canada College for five years, then after working with the Marlboros for a couple of years, I attended Boston College for a year. I returned to manage the Marlies. My son, Tommy, attended UCC as well, although he finished his high schooling at Jarvis Collegiate, just like his great-grandfather Conn. As Conn explained it to my father, an education at Upper Canada College was important because it taught boys that education was the great leveler, and that money and a famous name really were insignificant.

The entrepreneurial spirit is firmly ingrained in the Smythe blood. While at UCC I got an idea that would earn me a lot of spending money, but got me into a lot of trouble, too. Even though Upper Canada had a terrific sports store, I set up my own sports enterprise. I would bring home all the hockey sticks from Maple Leaf Gardens that were slightly cracked or chipped. Then I'd repair and sell them. At first, all the sales took place on campus to my schoolmates, but soon the word spread and I was standing at the nearby St. Clair subway station, selling reconditioned Leaf sticks to commuters. Fans just couldn't get enough. Imagine — a Maple Leaf custom stick. Demand quickly outstripped supply and I began raising the price every week. This was much better than the allowance I was getting at home. In fact, by the time I was 12 years old, I had purchased my first boat with earnings from broken Leaf sticks.

Then one morning when I arrived at school, there was a note stuck to my locker instructing me to report to the principal's office immediately. Naturally, I was somewhat worried as to what awaited; even more so when I walked in and saw my dad and the owners of the school's sports store were there. I relaxed slightly when I noted that Dad had a slight grin on his face. The principal didn't mince words, "Thomas, you're to stop selling your hockey sticks immediately. These men pay good, hard-earned money to operate a sports store on this campus, and you will not infringe on their livelihood. And just so you'll have an opportunity to think about your enterprise, you will serve four Saturday gatings. No further discussion." A gating-which imprisoned you in the study hall from 11 am to 1pm — was just about the worst punishment you could get. A Saturday gating was a detention of sorts.

As Dad and I walked out of the principal's office, I was prepared for a home punishment as well, but that smirk on Dad's face in the office should have tipped me off. There was no added discipline at home, and in fact, for one of the few times in my young life, I felt that my Dad was proud of me. He invited me to have my customers come down to Maple Leaf Gardens on Saturday mornings, setting me up in an empty area in the north-east corner to sell my broken Leaf sticks.

From the time I was very young, six or seven, I helped my dad and grandpa at the family gravel pit or at Conn's horse farm. I remember one summer day riding my bike more than two miles on the gravel road to get to work at Conn's farm. It was blazing hot, so I wore shorts. I arrived at the farm, tired and sweaty. Grandpa asked, "What the hell are you doing here in short pants?" I told him it was too hot to bicycle to work in long pants in the summer. Conn smirked, glanced over at 90 tons of straw that had just been delivered, pointed, and told me, "Ok then, get to work."

"Grandpa, can I go home and put on some long pants," I asked. "Uh uh," he replied. "If you're foolish enough to show up for work on a farm in shorts, then you'll face the consequences." I dug in, but the straw was sharp and my legs were soon bleeding. My grandmother, who was amazing at calming his anger, made Conn drive me home just after noon to change, but not before I'd learned a valuable lesson. My grandfather had a wicked temper that he wasn't afraid to unleash on family and foes alike, but with a few words from Irene, he settled right down. There was a lot of love between my grandmother and grandfather, with equal measures of respect.

One of my early passions was riding horses. I loved to be around Conn's stable, feeding, grooming and exercising the horses. Grandpa was pleased that I took an interest in his horses and that I became an accomplished rider. One summer, it was my job to help teach the yearlings how to come out of the starting gate to properly train them for race day. My grandfather assigned two jockeys to work with me. Conn's farm was not too far from Highway 10 in Caledon and one of my responsibilities was to make certain there were no loud trucks going by when the yearlings were in the gate. The noise would spook the horses and they'd bolt. On this particular day, I heard some trucks in the distance. While I was waiting for the vehicles to pass, I gripped the reins and sitting on the horse, leaned back so I was lying flat in the saddle. Conn happened to be in the area and saw what I was doing, so prepared to teach me a lesson. He quietly drove in, and signaled one of the jockeys to open the gate. Terrified, the horse threw me to the ground, and galloped off wildly from where I laid. It took me over an hour to retrieve the yearling and several weeks before the bruises dissolved. But you'd better believe I never did that again.

I was fired from the farm on various occasions, but never for too long. It's hard to say why my father and grandfather were so tough on me. Perhaps they both wanted to insure I didn't take the Smythe name for granted. Maybe it was because Conn had been fairly lenient with Stafford and regretted not being firmer. Dad was given all sorts of privileges from an early age-he drove a convertible as a teenager, and never wanted for anything.

Grandpa used to laugh when he told us the story of the car he drove in the mid-thirties. It was a new automobile, but got terrible gas mileage. As was Conn's style, he marched right back into the dealership to complain that the car's gas consumption was outrageous. The dealer was confused, but the mystery was soon solved. When he got home, Conn caught my Dad siphoning gas out of Irene's car and using it for his convertible. To save his money, my father had been pulling this stunt on both Conn's and Irene's cars. It was amazing how the gas consumption improved dramatically in both cars from that point on.

Although I didn't appreciate how tough Dad and Grandpa were on me back then, I thank them today. They made me a much better man for all the occasions I cursed them, and I know it gave me the strength to get through some extraordinarily challenging times.

Chapter Five

Ballard

Harold Ballard was a big, jolly soul — quick with a quip and fast with his fury. He was born in Toronto in 1903, and while growing up, his father established the Ballard Machinery Company. The company manufactured sewing machines for Toronto's textile trade. As a sideline, it also manufactured Ballard Rockered Tube Skates. I hate to debunk a longstanding myth, but although Harold claimed to be the 1920 Toronto speed skating champion, I've been told he was actually a poor skater.

Ballard did go to the Olympics, although not as an athlete. At the 1928 Winter games in St. Moritz Switzerland, the University of Toronto Varsity Grads were chosen to represent Canada in hockey. They had won the Ontario Hockey League's senior championship the year before, earning the right to represent their country. My grandfather, who had captained the Varsitys when he played for them, was coach of the team, but his recent purchase of the Toronto Maple Leafs tied up his time, and he was forced to decline his invitation to the international competition. In his place, W. A. Hewitt, Foster's father, was named coach and manager of the Varsitys. Hewitt had become secretary of the Ontario Hockey Association in 1903, doing much to shape the league during his more than 50 years with the OHA.

Harold Ballard was appointed assistant manager to help run the club.

When Canada's Olympic hopefuls arrived in St. Moritz, they needed to choose someone from their ranks to carry the Canadian flag in the parade of athletes. Amazingly, they chose, the 25-year-old Ballard, despite not being an Olympic athlete.

The team won all three games of the Olympic competition, beating Sweden 11-0, Britain 14-0 and Switzerland 13-0, earning a gold medal for Canada. While in Switzerland, Ballard stole the Olympic flag, a feat of which he was immensely proud. The U of T Varsity Grads returned to a hero's welcome back home in Toronto. They were paraded through the streets in front of thousands of patriotic fans. The parade concluded at Old City Hall, where the mayor and city council gave the team a civic reception. The Grads included several members who went on to further fame. Left winger Dave Trottier enjoyed a 10-year NHL career with the Montreal Maroons, and participated in the 1937 all-star game held to commemorate former Montreal star, Howie Morenz, who had died earlier that year. Hugh Plaxton, a centre for the Grads, had a brief stint in the NHL, also with the Maroons. Goalie Joe Sullivan later became a Canadian Senator — the political kind. And right-winger Dr. Lou Hudson has a more obscure hockey connection. It was his brother, Dr. Henry Hudson, who died in the August 1951 plane crash that claimed the life of Maple Leaf Bill Barilko, just months after he scored the Stanley Cup winning goal.

During the late 1920s, motorboat racing captured the imaginations of Toronto sports enthusiasts. The boats, which were actually small hydroplanes only 10 to 12 feet long and very light, became known as Sea Fleas for the way they flitted over the water. Toronto's National Yacht Club, which was located close to what is now Lakeshore Boulevard and Bathurst Street, became the home to the Sea Fleas, and regularly promoted races for the small boats. Harold embraced this new sport like he did most things fast and exciting during that era. A member of the NYC, Harold enjoyed racing the sea fleas, and was extremely competitive at it. The National Yacht Club regularly held races on Lake Ontario, with thousands of people lining the shoreline between what is now Ontario Place, east along the lakeshore to Sunnyside Park, where little but the Sunnyside Bathing Pavilion remains today.

The National Yacht Club sponsored a senior team in the Ontario Hockey Association, beginning in 1930-31. Harold was appointed business manager of the team, which was called the Toronto National Sea Fleas. The next season, the team won the Allan Cup as senior hockey's top team in Canada. It is well documented that the Toronto Maple Leafs and Chicago Blackhawks played the first game in Maple Leaf Gardens, a 2-1 win for Chicago. But the second game, a night after the Gardens' christening, was a 3-2 Toronto Nationals victory over the Toronto Marlboros.

Following the championship, Ballard took over as coach of the Sea Fleas partway through the 1932-33 season. But this time the team didn't make the playoffs. Many players quit after Harold was quoted in the newspapers as calling them "lazy." To salvage the disappointing season, Ballard took the Sea Fleas to Europe for two months, with the trip culminating in the Ice Hockey Federation world championship in Prague. The team easily beat its competitors in England, France, Germany and Austria, but off the ice, it got itself in all sorts of troubles.

In Paris, a champagne party back at the hotel ended in a skirmish. Harold Ballard ended up in jail, and it took the Canadian embassy to secure his release the next day. At the world championship in Prague, a Boston team representing the United States defeated the Sea Fleas. The 2-1 loss was the first time Canada had ever suffered a defeat at the Ice Hockey Federation world championship. When the team returned to Canada in disgrace, hockey's governing body, the Canadian Amateur Hockey Association, investigated it.

In 1934, the Sea Fleas merged with a west Toronto team to become the West Toronto Nationals, an OHA Junior team. Harold realized that he was a much better manager than coach and hired Clarence Hap Day to work behind the Nationals bench. Day was playing with the Leafs at the time, and when the NHL club's schedule conflicted with that of the Nationals, Ballard would replace Hap Day as the team's coach. In 1936, the team won the Memorial Cup as top junior team in Canada, defeating the Saskatoon Wesleys. Stars of the champion Nationals included the Conacher twins, Hall of Fame member Roy and his brother Bert, whose own hockey career was halted when he lost an eye in a street hockey accident with older brother Charlie, the Maple Leafs superstar.

Although Harold Ballard was already well known around Maple Leaf Gardens, he gradually worked his way into the Maple Leafs organization through his friendship with Day. Both Harold and Leaf coach Day lived in the west end of the city, and the two would drive in to the Gardens together each day. Ballard's big break came during the Second World War when Day suggested to Frank Selke, Conn's right hand man, that Ballard would make a good choice to run the Toronto Marlboros. Selke agreed, and appointed Ballard president and general manager of the Toronto Marlboros Junior hockey team.

The Toronto Marlborough Athletic Club was formed just after the turn of the century by a group of avid Toronto sports fans, including Fred Waghorne, who was later selected as an honoured member of the Hockey Hall of Fame in the Builders category. The Athletic Club chose the name "Marlboroughs" after the Duke of Marlborough, who was Sir Winston Churchill's uncle. Waghorne actually wrote the Duke, requesting permission for the club to use not only his title, but also his crest, and received his blessing. Through the years, the spelling was altered to "Marlboros," and a common nickname for the team was the "Dukes."

In 1904, the Athletic Club formed its own hockey team, and actually challenged the Ottawa Silver Seven for the Stanley Cup, although they were defeated.

Frank Selke's junior hockey roots went back to 1915, when Grandpa captained the Varsity Juniors in an Ontario junior semifinal series against Selke's Berlin Union Jacks. The city of Berlin later changed its name to Kitchener to avoid anti-German sentiment following World War I. Selke left Berlin, and headed the OHA Junior St. Mary's Saints. In 1926-27, Frank Selke moved to Toronto, and his St. Mary's Saints became the Toronto Marlboros. Hockey was a cottage industry for Selke, as he worked as an electrician at the University of Toronto during the day, and coached and managed the Marlboros and the Toronto Ravinas in the evenings and on weekends. Ravina Gardens was the name of the arena, long gone, where the Maple Leafs and Marlboros would practice for their games at Toronto's Arena Gardens, commonly known as the Mutual Street Arena. The Ravina Gardens was right beside Humberside Collegiate in Toronto's High Park area.

When my grandfather purchased the Toronto St. Pats in 1927, he needed a supply of strong, young talent, and Frank Selke was acknowledged as being one of the best in the country at developing young hockey players. Grandpa had been well aware of Selke's hockey abilities, and many times through the years offered financial help to his Ravinas. Conn later secured the Toronto Marlboros as part of the Maple Leaf organization, a move that paid huge dividends throughout the years. With the Marlboros, my grandfather brought Frank Selke to the organization, keeping him on as coach as well as giving him the job as assistant general manager with the Maple Leafs and a position at the gravel pit. In 1927-28, the Marlboros went to the Eastern final; a step away from the Memorial Cup final, and the following year, Toronto was victorious. Coach Frank Selke, along with Conn as vice-president, Harvey Jackson, Charlie Conacher and Reginald Red Horner, the Marlboros captured the Memorial Cup as Junior champions. Just four years later, Jackson, Conacher and Horner would lead the NHL's Maple Leafs to their first Stanley Cup victory. Before the Marlboros disbanded following the 1988-89 season, they had won seven Memorial Cup championships-more than any other team in Canadian Junior Hockey history.

The Toronto Maple Leafs won the Stanley Cup in 1941-42, coming back from a three-game-to-zero deficit in the final series versus Detroit. With their fourth straight victory, the Maple Leafs celebrated their miraculous Cup victory with the traditional party of champagne-soaked superlatives. Ballard stood elbow to elbow in the dressing room with Hap Day, Syl Apps, Turk Broda and the rest of the victors, commemorating the occasion.

When my father returned home from World War II, he and Ballard renewed their acquaintance. Before the war, Stafford had actually played hockey on a team managed by Ballard. Although Harold was 18 years older than Dad, closer to my grandfather's age than my father's, he and Stafford became fast friends. "Fast" may be a very appropriate word to describe their relationship, as the two commonly enjoyed the more affluent things in life together.

As is the case with many good partnerships, both friends had distinctly different personalities, and that may well have been what drew them together. Dad was quite serious and businesslike, but loved to laugh at Harold's amusing banter. Together, Stafford coached while Harold managed the Junior Toronto Marlboros. My father quickly found his calling in the operations side of the team, while Harold's callings were more on the business side.

By the early fifties, Dad was the managing director of the Toronto Marlboros, while Harold took on the presidency. The two of them were inseparable. Mom and Dad socialized extensively with Harold and his wife Dorothy. The Ballards lived on Montgomery Road in Etobicoke — a prestigious suburb on the western edge of Toronto — and we lived just a couple of minutes away on Edgehill Road. Many Leaf players and executives lived in this area of Toronto, including Red Kelly, Billy Harris, Johnny Bower as well as Harold and my dad. Etobicoke's Kingsway area was not only — and still is — one of Toronto's most affluent communities, but also was located halfway between Maple Leaf Gardens and the airport.

We Smythe children looked at Harold and Dorothy Ballard as our second parents, and I would imagine that Mary Elizabeth, Bill and Bobby Ballard felt the same about my mother and father.

It was an exciting time around Maple Leaf Gardens after the war. The Maple Leafs won the Stanley Cup in 1946-47, 1947-48, 1948-49 and 1950-51 under my grandfather. With Harold Ballard and my father running the team, the Junior A Marlboros won the Memorial Cup in 1954-55 and 1955-56. The Leafs other Junior affiliate, St. Michael's College, won the Memorial Cup in 1946-47. And in 1949-50, the Toronto Marlboros Senior team won the Allan Cup under Harold Ballard.

During his years associated with the Toronto Maple Leafs and Maple Leaf Gardens, right up until his death in 1990, Ballard was known for his obscure antics. In 1979, following a 2-1 loss to the Leafs rival Canadiens, Ballard fired head coach Roger Neilson, only to reinstate him 2 days later when a replacement had not been found. Reports of Neilson's firing were all over the sports pages and the Leaf players, the Toronto fans and reporters alike were all curious to see who would step behind the Leaf bench for their March 3rd game against the Flyers.

Ballard attempted to convince Neilson to wear a paper bag over his head as he walked to the bench in an effort to keep the arena in suspense regarding his identity. I can't imagine the president of an NHL franchise would attempt to impose such embarrassment on, and undermine the authority of a member of his coaching staff.

In that same season, the NHL announced John Ziegler as the leagues newest president. One of Ziegler's earliest legislative moves was to impose a rule forcing all teams to display the player's names on the back of their jersey's. He felt that this would allow the fans and media greater ease to identify the players. Ballard was concerned that these prominently displayed names would jeopardize the sale of his game programs and flat-out ignored the rule. When he was fined $2,000 for each game the Leafs remained nameless, Ballard finally recognize the rule, however in spite, had the names stitched in the same colour as the jersey's, rendering them useless. In time, the Leafs followed the rule and the team sweaters conformed to meet the new NHL's standards.

It wasn't just hockey where Ballard would make outlandish moves. During a concert at the Gardens in the 60s, Ballard raised the air temperature and shut down many of the water fountains around the building. This move allowed him to generate huge profits at the concessions stands.

Chapter Six

Junior Hockey

As Conn grew older, the recurring pain in his back and right leg grew worse. My grandfather had been badly wounded in World War II and was never quite the same afterwards. Conn was in constant pain for the rest of his life. As Grandpa's health declined, so did the fortunes of the Toronto Maple Leafs.

The Leafs had a tough decade in the 1950s. The team won the Stanley Cup in 1950-51 on a dramatic overtime goal by Bill Barilko. It was on April 21, 1951, and Barilko, a five-year Toronto veteran, picked up a rebound and lifted a backhand over the right shoulder of Montreal Canadiens goaltender Gerry McNeil at 2:53 of overtime to give the Leafs the Stanley Cup. Toronto won the series four games to one, with each of the five games being decided in overtime. It was the first and still is the only time a Stanley Cup series had each game decided in an overtime period. Later that summer, on August 26, Bill Barilko and his friend Dr. Henry Hudson, a Timmins dentist, were killed when their single engine pontoon plane crashed while they were on a fishing trip in northern Ontario. It was 11 years before the bodies were discovered and ironically, 11 years before the Toronto Maple Leafs would win another Stanley Cup.

After winning the 1950-51 Stanley Cup with the infamous Barilko overtime goal, the Leafs were knocked out of the playoffs in the semi-finals versus Detroit in 1951-52. Toronto missed the playoffs entirely the next season. They were defeated by the Red Wings in the semi-finals again in 1953-54. Detroit dumped the Leafs from the playoffs again in the 1954-55 semi-finals. In 1955-56, the Detroit Red Wings again defeated the Maple Leafs in the semi-finals. The 1956-57 season ended with Toronto out of the playoffs, and the results were even worse the next year when the Leafs finished dead last.

There was a marked improvement in 1958-59, the first year with Punch Imlach as coach, as Toronto pushed past the Boston Bruins in the semi-finals, only to fall to the Canadiens in the finals. The 1959-60 playoffs saw the Maple Leafs defeat the Wings in the semi-finals, but the Montreal juggernaut rolled over Toronto in the finals.

The Smythe family sand and gravel operation, originally named C. Smythe For Sand, (or, as my grandpa preferred, See Smythe for Sand) had not only been the foundation of Conn's fortunes, but had been a source of summer income for many Leaf players from the 1930s through to the '50s. Name any Leaf from that era, and chances are pretty good that my grandfather had him driving a truck or shoveling gravel. Hap Day, Turk Broda, Bob Goldham and Tim Horton are just a few who built up their physiques by working for Conn during the summer. My dad, Stafford, was no different: he had worked in the family sand and gravel business for years.

C. Smythe for Sand was located in Toronto's west-end just down from Scarlett Road, above St. Clair. When my grandfather purchased the property in 1920, it had been farmland, and Conn was able to buy acres for a pittance. The land yielded tons and tons of both sand and gravel, and my Grandpa's business expanded quickly. When I was born, Mom and Dad lived at the top of a hill near the sandpit on a street called East Drive. When the land had surrendered all the sand and gravel it contained, Conn sold much of the property, and an entire subdivision was built on the old gravel pit. Grandpa also donated enough land to create a tranquil park for the city. Named Smythe Park, it's a beautiful, peaceful place full of geese and a flowing creek. There is a pool, and next to the tennis courts is a large boulder with a plaque from the Aggregate Producers Association of Ontario that reads: "Presented June 14th, 1977 to Mr. Conn Smythe and to the Borough of York to commemorate the origin of these grounds and their transformation from a gravel pit into an outstanding recreational area with considerable environmental appeal and a distinct asset to the community."

Once the Scarlett Road sand and gravel pit had been exhausted of its resources, Conn began buying up hundreds of acres of property in Caledon Township. Although they maintained the home at 68 Baby Point Road as their principal residence, Conn and Irene eventually had a house, a horseracing stable and the sand and gravel pit all located northwest of the city. Caledon was vast and quiet, and we looked forward to visiting Grandma and Grandpa there.

Stafford had a number of talents that made him valuable to Conn. Even as an 11-year-old minor hockey player, he coached and managed his own team. While attending the University of Toronto, Stafford coached and managed the university's hockey team. From the time Dad was 10, he was stickboy for the Leafs, including that incredible first year in Maple Leaf Gardens when the Leafs won the Stanley Cup, defeating a New York Ranger team that Conn had helped assemble before purchasing the Toronto St. Pats. These experiences prepared Dad well for his work with the Toronto Marlboros, then later with the Toronto Maple Leafs.

Through the 1930s and 1940s, the Maple Leafs were fed talented hockey players by their two Toronto Junior teams, the Marlboros and St. Michael's College. For the most part, the junior players were divided by religion. Roman Catholic players attended St. Michael's College, which was run by the Basilican Fathers. Protestant boys played for the Marlboros. Most of the players were from outside Toronto; a surprisingly large number of players came from northern Ontario. Dad vowed to find more boys from the Toronto area who could play either for the Marlies or St. Mike's, some of whom might go on to play for the Leafs.

My father helped set up the Marlboro minor hockey network in the early 1950s. The system scouted boys as young as nine years old and fed them into the Leaf system, hoping that a few would make the climb all the way from peewee, upwards through the organization and, if good enough, end up on either the St. Michael's Majors or the Toronto Marlboros. A few, Dad hoped, would join the Toronto Maple Leafs roster one-day.

Several players, including Bobby Baun, Carl Brewer, Bob Pulford and Billy Harris, were successful results of the Marlboro system. Each had been discovered on rinks around Toronto as teenagers, placed on the Marlboro peewee or bantam team, and had worked their way up to play for the Junior A Marlboros. Then, they graduated to the parent team itself — the Toronto Maple Leafs.

I, too, had been in the Marlboro system as a teenager, but I was neither big enough nor good enough to play professionally, and my formal hockey career ended in Junior B. I once played on a hockey team with Hockey Hall of Fame inductee and the current president of the Maple Leafs, Ken Dryden. I often obscure the fact that we were only seven years old at the time. In 1954, my father and his friend Jack Stafford Jr. decided that they wanted to give their children an opportunity to play hockey in the Etobicoke area. They got the word out, and in the league's first year, Humber Valley had two teams for players 10 years of age or under — the Hornets and the Redmen. Ken Dryden was our goalie on the Redmen, where I played right wing. As a special treat, my grandfather allowed the Hornets and Redmen to play a game at Maple Leaf Gardens. It was an incredible memory for two seven-year-olds.

The hockey world is so small. Jack Stafford Jr. comes from the family that owned Stafford Specialty Foods, a company that made chocolate syrups and other confections. Silver Seven, committee member George Mara had actually played OHA Senior hockey with Jack Stafford Jr. on the Toronto Staffords in 1944-45. The Staffords were named after the food company, and had nothing to do with my father. The team included former Leaf players Normie Mann, Rhys Thomson and Jack McLean, as well as future Leaf captain Sid Smith. Jack Stafford Sr. was president and general manager. Red Horner coached the team.

Dad and his team of scouts were very good at their jobs, and their clever detective work paid huge dividends. The Toronto Marlboro Major Junior A team won back-to-back Memorial Cups in 1954-55 and 1955-56 with Dad as the managing director and Harold Ballard as president. The Marlies also won in 1963-64, 1966-67, 1972-73 and 1974-75. St. Michael's Majors won the Memorial Cup in 1960-61. Several of the Marlboro graduates, joined by some St. Michael's College graduates, later helped the Leafs win those four Stanley Cups in the 1960s.

Dad had an amazing eye for talent. I don't think people ever really gave him enough credit for his uncanny ability to spot potential NHL players as young as 12 years old. Stafford had been groomed to take over the Toronto Maple Leafs and Maple Leaf Gardens just like I had. With his successes at the junior level, Dad was well prepared to move up to the professional ranks and, as the decade unfolded, he pushed to be more involved in the running of the Toronto Maple Leafs.

Chapter Seven

The Silver Seven

Clarence Hap Day had played defense for Toronto between 1924-25 and 1936-37. He pre-dated the Maple Leafs, playing for the Toronto St. Patricks for two seasons. The St. Pats had struggled during the 1926 season, and they offered my grandfather the opportunity to manage the team. J. P. Bickell, one of the owners, called Conn with the offer, but Grandpa didn't bite. "Look, Jack. I just put together the New York Rangers for Tex Rickard and he screwed me by hiring Lester Patrick to take my place," Conn fumed. "I came to you for a job with the St. Pats and you hired Mike Rodden instead. Said I didn't have enough pro experience." Well, look how well Rodden did. He's gone, and now you're calling me to reconsider. Jack, the only way I'd be interested is if I could buy a part of the team. There's no way in hell I'm going through that crap again — working my butt off, only to be at the mercy of some owner's whims."

The team had considered a move to Philadelphia, but my grandfather argued vehemently that a move away from Toronto would be devastating for the city. J.P. Bickell felt that Conn could buy the team for $200,000 — the amount Philadelphia had offered. "Look Conny. I own one-fifth of the team. I'll leave my $40,000 with the organization, on the condition that you can come up with the remaining $160,000 to buy out my partners," negotiated Bickell. My Grandfather found enough interested investors, and bought the St. Pats in February 1927.

Conn christened the team the Maple Leafs. Grandpa always told us that he chose "Maple Leafs" as the team's name in honour of the maple leaf insignia he had worn during the First World War. But there had been a Toronto Maple Leafs hockey team in the first decade of last century. Those, Toronto Maple Leafs played in the Ontario Professional League, and challenged the Montreal Wanderers for the Stanley Cup in 1908. There had also been a Toronto Maple Leafs baseball team in the International League as early as 1912. My grandfather also decided to change the hockey team's colours from green and white to the now famous blue and white. Only two of the St. Pats players actually went on to star with the Maple Leafs — Ace Bailey and Hap Day.

Once the Leafs were in their new building, Grandpa lorded over it, wearing his ever-present spats and sporting a morning coat. With his formal attire, my grandfather looked more like he was going to his own wedding than he did a hockey game. Long before arenas had glass, Conn would walk along the top of the boards, speaking to the fans. He was also checking that the crowd was dressed in proper attire (jacket and tie for the gentlemen) and was behaving properly. And there was no smoking, drinking or throwing allowed. If you broke the rules once, you were warned; brake them twice and your season's tickets were revoked. Thus, Conn ensured that Maple Leaf Garden's crowds were always well mannered and well dressed.

Hap was the first captain of the Toronto Maple Leafs. He had been a fabulous defenseman for the Toronto franchise for 13 seasons between 1924 and 1937 — two with the St. Pats and 11 as a Leaf. Although he was traded to the New York Americans in 1937 at the conclusion of his playing career, Day was brought back to coach the Leafs for the 1940-41 season, and stayed on as coach until the conclusion of the playoffs in the spring of 1950. During his tenure, Hap coached the Leafs to five Stanley Cups — more than any other Leaf coach in history. Because of his excellence as a player, Clarence Hap Day was inducted into the Hockey Hall of Fame in 1961.

In 1950, Day was given the opportunity to manage the team. Former Maple Leaf Kid Line star, Joe Primeau, was brought in to coach the Leafs, and he did for three seasons between 1950 and 1953. King Clancy, who coached for three seasons between 1953 and 1956, followed Primeau. For the 1956-57 season, another former Leaf star, Howie Meeker, was hired as coach. Although Conn didn't surrender the title of general manager, it was Hap who really held the position.

Stafford pushed Conn to relinquish the running of the Leafs. He felt the team's fortunes would turn around by bringing in a new, more youthful attitude in management. Finally, my grandfather agreed to allow Stafford to set up a hockey committee that would help plan and rebuild the future for the Leafs and in 1957, the "Silver Seven", as they came to be known, was born. The Silver Seven had but one goal in mind: to bring the Stanley Cup back to Toronto.

The group was comprised of my father, Stafford Smythe, Jack Amell, John Bassett, George Gardiner, Bill Hatch, George Mara and Ian Johnson. Harold Ballard, who had run the Marlboro farm system with my father, soon replaced Johnson. All seven were avid hockey fans and had been friends for a number of years. Jack Amell was vice-president of Robert Amell and Company, a jewelry manufacturing company. He owned the cottage next to my grandfather on Lake Simcoe. John Bassett Jr. was publisher of the daily Toronto Telegram newspaper and owned CFTO-TV in Toronto. George Gardiner was president of Gardiner, Watson Limited, a stock brokerage firm. Bill Hatch was a vice-president at McLaren's Food Products. And George Mara had played junior and senior hockey in Toronto, won a gold medal with the Canadian Olympic hockey team in 1948, and was the third generation to hold North American rights to Beefeater Gin. He was president of William Mara and Company, and imported alcohol and wine into Canada.

John Bassett Jr. had asked my grandfather about the possibility of his joining the Maple Leafs board of directors as early as 1953. My grandfather had known the Bassett family for decades. John Bassett Sr. had been on the board of directors of the old Ottawa Senators in the late 1920s until the team moved to St. Louis in 1934, and Conn knew the senior Bassett from back then. John Bassett Jr. had been involved with the junior team in Sherbrooke, and knew Stafford through his work with the Marlboros. He was invited to join the board of directors of Maple Leaf Gardens in 1953. My dad was made a director in 1956. Amell, Gardiner, Hatch and Mara all became directors in 1958. Harold Ballard joined the board in 1961. The seven worked hard at scouting young players and looking for opportunities to help the Maple Leafs through trades.

The hockey committee met weekly and frequently traveled with the Leafs on the road. The Silver Seven discussed draft choices and argued about trades. Some journalists questioned the viability of the Silver Seven, as stories of the group's carousing became legendary. But through clever trades and an outstanding farm system, the fortunes of the Toronto Maple Leafs would drastically change from the poor showing in the fifties, and the team would go on to win four Stanley Cups under the leadership of the Silver Seven.

The Silver Seven knew that the Leafs in the spring of 1957, were in trouble. The team had finished in fifth place that year, missing the playoffs entirely. My dad and the others on the hockey committee felt that the team was being blocked from growing by Hap Day's refusal to change both the style of his management and the defensive style of the team. The Silver Seven theorized that Day's system was antiquated, and my

Grandfather, recognizing that he had given the hockey committee the opportunity to show that they could reverse the Leafs downward spiral, couldn't take away their right to that opinion. At a press conference held in New York, Conn carefully but deliberately let the press know that the Leafs system was out of date, but that Day was still the general manager and was going to be asked if he was still available to manage the team. The Toronto sportswriters had a field day with that one sentence, reading between the lines that the owner was questioning Day's abilities. Day himself was livid and met with Conn privately in Toronto. Being asked if he was "still available" after serving the Toronto Maple Leafs for over 30 years undermined Day's position, and he resigned. Day, former Leaf star and captain, Stanley Cup-winning coach and general manager, and manager and minority owner of Conn Smythe's sand and gravel business, was now on the outside of the Toronto Maple Leaf organization. And yet, my Grandpa always considered him the best friend he ever had.

The area of immediate concern for the Silver Seven was replacing Day as manager. My dad had come forward with the name of a successful minor league hockey manager as his recommendation for the position. The previous year, this gentleman had coached and managed the underdog Springfield Indians to the finals in the American Hockey League. His name was George "Punch" Imlach.

Maple Leafs' management had known of Imlach since the late 1930s. Imlach, a Toronto boy, had played Junior A hockey with the Toronto Young Rangers, who practiced early mornings in the Gardens. Later, playing senior hockey with the Toronto Goodyears, George Imlach earned the nickname "Punchy" (later shortened to Punch) after an on-ice scrap in Windsor, Ontario. During World War II, Imlach served in the Army, returning after the war to Quebec City where he played, later coached and managed and eventually, partially owned the Aces of the

Quebec Senior Hockey League. During his years in Quebec, Imlach had signed Jean Beliveau to a contract with the Aces. In 1957-58, Punch joined the Boston Bruins organization, where he was assigned to Springfield under the dictatorial ownership of former Bruins all-star, Eddie Shore.

My grandfather still retained the general manager's title with the Maple Leafs. This was of monumental concern to Punch, who wanted both control and the title. When Conn assured him that he'd have his control but would have to earn the general manager's mantle over the course of time, Imlach finally backed down and accepted the position as assistant general manager.

Billy Reay, a former Montreal Canadiens forward, had coached 20 games into a losing 1958-59 season when Imlach was called before the Silver Seven to discuss the problems with the team. Punch felt that a change had to be made, but as assistant manager, didn't have the authority to fire Reay. The hockey committee went to Conn and asked that he give Imlach the general manager's title. Grandpa finally agreed, and Punch Imlach became the new general manager of the Toronto Maple Leafs. His first duty was to fire Billy Reay.

Without a replacement on hand, Imlach stepped behind the bench and coached the Leafs. Both Imlach and the Silver Seven searched for an appropriate replacement for Reay, but continually came up empty. At one point, Alf Pike, a former Rangers player coaching in the junior ranks, was considered. But it was Conn who decided Punch should stand behind the bench as interim coach. For the remainder of that season, and the next ten as well, Imlach was coach and general manager of the Toronto Maple Leafs. Both my grandpa and dad felt that this decision laid the foundation that not only turned around the team's fortunes, but also helped propel the Leafs to some of the greatest successes in its history.

Another area addressed by the Silver Seven was goaltending. Ed Chadwick had been a steady force in net, but the committee didn't feel confident that he had the talent to take the team to the Stanley Cup. The recommendation was to secure the services of Johnny Bower. Bower had been a longtime minor league goaltender, playing with a strong Cleveland Barons team in the American Hockey League from 1945 to 1953. In the 1940s and '50s, each NHL team carried just one goalie, so there were only six goaltending positions available in the NHL. Today, with 30 teams and each with at least two and often three goalies on the roster, 60 to 70 netminders have earned NHL employment. Bower had been saddled with the reputation of being an excellent AHL goalie who had likely risen to the level of his own ability, and had accepted that he was unlikely to play in the NHL. Then, during the summer of 1953, the New York Rangers made a trade with Cleveland and added Bower to their roster. Remarkably, Johnny Bower would be replacing Gump Worsley in the Rangers net, in spite of the fact that Gump had been selected as the best NHL rookie that year, winning the Calder Trophy for the 1952-53, season.

Johnny Bower played the full 1953-54, season with the Rangers, but at the beginning of the following season, he and Gump traded positions once again. This time, Worsley returned to the NHL club while Johnny took his spot with the Ranger's Western Hockey League club in Vancouver. In 1955-56, Johnny Bower returned to his old familiar league, the AHL, where he played with the Providence Reds for two seasons, then joined his friends on the Cleveland Barons once again for the 1957-58, season. Bower was sensational. When the 1957-58 campaign wound down, Johnny was first team AHL all-star goaltender (the fifth time he had been selected). He also won the AHL award for fewest goals against (he won that award three times) and was the AHL's most valuable player, a feat he accomplished three times. When the inter-league draft was held during the summer of 1958, the Silver Seven grabbed Johnny Bower for the Toronto Maple Leafs.

Johhny Bower remembers meeting my grandfather after the Stanley Cup victory in 1961-62. Conn cornered Johnny in the hallway of Maple Leaf Gardens. "John, you played some great goal this spring," Conn began. "I certainly hope we'll see you back here in the fall."

"Well, Mr. Smythe," started Bower. "I own a coffee shop in Wakabash up near Prince Albert, and maybe it's time for me to spend some time there."

"Nonsense," roared my grandfather. "If I don't see you strapping on your goal pads at training camp this fall, I'll throw a bomb into that little coffee shop of yours." Conn was obviously kidding, but his point was made: the Leafs weren't going to continue winning hockey games without a goaltender named Johnny Bower.

Bower returned to the Leafs for the 1962-63 season and each season following until his retirement in 1970. He was inducted into the Hockey Hall of Fame in 1976 for his incredible goaltending abilities and startling career goals against average of 2.52.

Chapter Eight

Power Struggle

The seven members of the Silver Seven hockey committee were chomping at the bit to wrestle more control away from my grandfather. The word "ownership" was beginning to spring from the lips of the directors with surprising regularity. In fact, my father Stafford, Harold Ballard and John Bassett, all members of the Silver Seven, had made Conn a $4-million offer to buy the Leafs and the Gardens in 1958, but my grandfather turned them down. But by 1961, Stafford and Conn were at each other's throats. Stafford was 40 years old, and had proven himself a savvy hockey administrator, both with the Marlboros and as chairman of the Silver Seven hockey committee. Prodded by his partners, he wanted what he felt was rightfully his-the Toronto Maple Leafs and Maple Leaf Gardens. Conn was not prepared to relinquish his role as owner, even though his health was diminishing, and at 66 years of age, other diversions like racehorses and charity work were taking up more and more of his time.

Finally, after three days of haggling, my grandfather issued a challenge. "Look Staff, I'll agree to sell you the Gardens, but it's on my terms, do you understand? I own over 50,000 shares, and I'll sell you 45,000 of them. But I want $40 a share. That's just over market value. You come up with that amount, in cash, and I'll sell you the Gardens."

Unknown to Conn at the time, Stafford had made a deal with Ballard and Bassett to raise the money. Although my father didn't have the money, Ballard felt he could come up with $2-million towards the purchase of the Gardens. The two spent the night poring over the Maple Leaf Gardens' financial records to analyze how successful the organization could be. In the morning, Stafford went to work at the gravel pit, and Ballard went to work on the bank manager at his branch of the Bank of Nova Scotia. After some negotiations, Ballard called my Dad to meet him at the bank. The loan had been approved and there were papers that needed signing.

Dad felt that the two longtime partners could buy Maple Leaf Gardens on their own, but Ballard stood firm and insisted that the team was comprised of three members, not two, and that John Bassett would be a third owner. Bassett, a war veteran like Conn and Stafford, was a very ambitious sort. In addition to his ownership of the Toronto Telegram and Baton Broadcasting, Bassett had an ownership role in the Toronto Argonauts football club and now, looked to be a part owner of the Toronto Maple Leafs and Maple Leaf Gardens.

Together, the three arranged the financing to offer my grandfather approximately $2.3 million, giving them almost 60% ownership of the Leafs and the Gardens. At the time, the Gardens' shares were selling for $33 apiece. The Stafford Smythe, Harold Ballard, John Bassett triumvirate would be paying the equivalent of $40 per share. Each of the partners would own approximately 20% of the stock. And an agreement was made that if any partner died or wished to sell his third those shares would first have to be offered to the other two partners.

Dad and Grandpa struck their deal with a firm handshake. Conn understood that he was making the deal with his son, Stafford, exclusively, and that some day, Stafford would make a similar deal with me so I could continue as the third generation of Smythes to run the Toronto Maple Leaf hockey club and Maple Leaf Gardens. Dad assured Conn that he would operate the organization with the same integrity that Conn had — it would be business as usual, and none of my grandfather's loyal employees would lose their jobs.

Stafford had always wanted to own a Cadillac. After his purchase of Maple Leaf Gardens, Dad finally purchased his dream car. It was gorgeous — palomino caramel — coloured exterior and interior, with big fins on the back that identified the Cadillacs of the 1960s. My father wanted a new car every year, so on his lunch hour when he was ready for a trade-in, he'd stroll along Carlton, past Yonge Street where Carlton becomes College, then over to Addison's on Bay Street. He'd walk over to Mr. Addison and tell him, "Order me a new Cadillac, and make it the same as last year's." The car would be the latest model, but was always the same colour inside and out.

A few days after the sale of the Gardens, Conn was told that his shares had not been sold solely to Stafford, but to his partners Harold Ballard and John Bassett as well. Grandpa hit the roof. "If I had had any idea that Ballard and Bassett were involved, I'd have cancelled the sale." John Bassett's Toronto Telegram edition of November 23, 1961, splashed the news across the front page: Change of Control for The Gardens. My grandfather was heartbroken. He felt deceived by his own son, whom he believed to be giving away two-thirds of the Smythe legacy.

Conn also felt that Dad had compromised my future. He knew that Harold Ballard and John Bassett both had children who now, potentially, would be in line to take over the Gardens and the Leafs one day. And that might, conceivably, leave me on the outside of the Gardens looking in. Since birth, my father and grandfather had prepared me for my destined role in Leaf ownership and now that destiny was uncertain.

Before the purchase of Grandpa's shares, Dad, Harold and John Bassett owned about 42,000 shares. With the purchase of Conn's 45,000, the three now owned around 87,000 shares. My dad was elected president of Maple Leaf Gardens. Harold Ballard became executive vice-president and John Bassett was chosen chairman of the board.

I have to admit that Harold did an amazing job of increasing revenues for Maple Leaf Gardens. When my grandfather was running the Gardens, revenue came from Leaf games, junior hockey receipts, and, at various times, lacrosse and basketball games, weekly wrestling cards, some political rallies, religious events and the odd musical program. The Gardens was busy, but there were a lot of what were called "dark nights" or non-operating days.

But when Harold took over that function, he increased the number of events held in the Gardens exponentially. As rock 'n roll gained popularity, Harold embraced the new genre, and booked many of the big acts who were going on tour. He also experimented with closed-circuit boxing matches.

For better or worse, Ballard re-configured much of the Gardens as well. In 1962, 981 new seats were added to bring the capacity of MLG up to 13,718. This was done by reducing the size of the seats and by finding new areas to construct seating. Unfortunately, many of the added seats were at the expense of Queen Elizabeth's picture, which hung prominently and was a focal point for players during the singing of our national anthem. Also removed was the organ loft and Foster Hewitt's broadcast location, the gondola. Up to that point, the best seats in the house had been "reds," the seats that ringed the ice level. Harold changed the colour of these seats to "golds," and moved the reds higher up in the stands. A premium price was charged for both.

Another innovation Ballard brought to the Gardens was advertising. Sponsors were found to advertise up the stairs and on the bottom of the seats in MLG. I think it's so ironic that Harold balked at selling advertising on the boards and ice for so long, making Maple Leaf Gardens one of the last arenas in the NHL to exploit this area of revenue generation. Following the introduction of board signage in 1989, MLG generated revenues averaging $250,000 per season, per board.

Finally, Harold had the Hot Stove Lounge constructed on the Church Street side of Maple Leaf Gardens. This was an exclusive restaurant and bar which was partially subsidized by the initiation fees and annual dues paid by season ticket holders. The rest of the profits came from the pricey meals and drinks served before and during games.

Thanks in great part to Harold's creative foresight, along with an era of outstanding hockey, the profits of Maple Leaf Gardens grew from $300,000 in 1961 to $900,000 just three years later. Shares in the Gardens rose from $26.50 in 1961 to $114.75 in 1965, just before the stock split five for one.

Chapter Nine

The Flag

During the summer, my wife Penny and I enjoy our weekends at the cottage we own on Lake Simcoe. People visiting the area continually ask us about the huge blue-and-white Maple Leaf flag that flies proudly over our property. They wonder what it's all about and where it came from. This flag, a replica of the Canadian flag but in blue, first flew over Toronto City Hall after the Toronto Maple Leafs won the Stanley Cup in 1961-62. And it flew over City Hall three more times — each time the Leafs brought the Stanley Cup back to Toronto.

My dad often spoke to me with concern over the debt load he was carrying. It was, in part, a consequence of his focus on winning a Stanley Cup. Certainly the annual success it epitomizes in the NHL was part of the draw. And it was also the dream of every youngster growing up with an interest in hockey. But a third reason for the obsession was that a Stanley Cup victory would produce a large profit for the Toronto Maple Leaf organization, and in the process, greatly reduce Dad's debt.

After finishing dead last in 1957-58, the Toronto fans began to see some light at the end of the tunnel during the 1958-59 season. With Punch Imlach in place behind the bench, and with newly acquired Johnny Bower in net, the Leafs became an impressive opponent in 1958-59. Some of the players Stafford had developed in the Leafs system were beginning to make their marks. Frank Mahovlich was turning into a star contributor on the wing. Billy Harris was becoming an exceptional checking centre with offensive skills. Bob Pulford had developed into a strong forward with two-way skills and Carl Brewer looked like he had all-star capabilities in 1958-59, his first full season in the NHL. With the youngsters added to a line-up that included veterans George Armstrong, Dick Duff and Ron Stewart at forward and hard rocks Tim Horton and Bobby Baun on defense, the future looked very bright.

Punch also brought some new blood to the team through trades and drafts, and these players infused a new energy into the Leafs, as well as add veteran moxy. Gerry Ehman had played for Punch in the past, both in Quebec and in Springfield, and although he had only played in a handful of NHL games, he was an AHL first team all-star forward the previous year. Allan Stanley was added for defensive strength. Stanley had played ten NHL seasons already for the Rangers, Hawks and Bruins and his leadership and skills would become invaluable to the Leafs. Bert Olmstead was a no-nonsense forward who had won three Stanley Cups with Montreal before joining Toronto. He was a true leader, never hesitant to say what he felt on the bench or in the dressing room. Between periods of one game, Olmstead was especially fired up, and stood on the seats with his skate laces loosened, chastising his teammates for their lackadaisical effort. Out of the corner of his eye, Olmstead saw Bob Pulford whispering to Frank Mahovlich. Olmstead ripped off one of his skates and hurled it like a tomahawk at Pulford. Without batting an eye, Pulford's hand darted up and caught the skate mid-flight. "Don't tell me I'm not focused," blurted Pulford, and he tossed the skate at Olmstead's feet. Although Olmstead's methods may not have always been well calculated, his drive to win was evident and each player gained focus from his dedication.

There have been stranger deals I'm sure in the NHL, but I doubt that many compare to how Toronto acquired Bert Olmstead in June 1958. The Montreal Canadiens had left the veteran unprotected in the inter-league draft, and Toronto was quick to claim the services of Olmstead in exchange for cash. But a side deal was also prepared. Frank Selke, who had left the Leafs and my grandfather in a power struggle before the 1946-47 season, became the managing director of the Montreal Canadiens and stayed there for decades. Selke was instrumental in constructing the Habs dynasty of the 1950s. But Selke also bred boxer dogs, and had become somewhat successful in that venture. He sold many that went on to win prestigious awards at dog shows. When the Olmstead deal was being finalized, Stafford insisted that Selke throw in one of his prize-winning boxers as part of the deal. He refused at first, but finally agreed when Dad said. "No dog, no deal." Dad and Mom went to Montreal to pick out their new pet from the most recent litter. The puppy came back to Toronto with them, and Duke, named after the Toronto Marlboros nickname, became the newest family member at the Smythe household.

The new-look Leafs snuck into the playoffs with a victory in the final regular season game. It gave Toronto 65 points, one more than the New York Rangers. In the first round of the playoffs, the Leafs startled the second-place Bruins, knocking Boston out in seven games. In the finals, an excited Toronto team gave Montreal a good series, but eventually lost to the powerful Habs in five games.

There was much reason for optimism for the 1959-60 season. The nucleus from the previous season was retained. The only real change of note came late in the season. The Maple Leafs were able to pick up Red Kelly from Detroit for spare defenseman Marc Reaume. Kelly had been a perennial all-star in Detroit, chosen for the first team six times and the second team twice. Always considered an outstanding offensive defenseman, Imlach had a hunch that Red could be a more valuable asset to Toronto as a centre. By season's end, the Leafs had climbed to a solid second-place finish. In the semi-finals, Toronto pushed aside a pesky Red Wing team. In the finals though, the Leafs lost to the Canadiens once again. This was the fifth Stanley Cup in a row for Montreal; a dynasty that still stands as the most successful in NHL history.

The Maple Leafs battled Montreal for first place all season long in 1960-61. Frank Mahovlich had a sensational season, scoring 48 goals. Now playing centre, Red Kelly was second on the Leafs in scoring. Horton, Stanley, Olmstead, Duff and Armstrong continued to play outstanding hockey. Three new faces to the team that year were fan favourites Dave Keon, Bob Nevin and Eddie Shack. Bobby Nevin had come up through the Marlboro system, and finally got his shot in 1960-61. Dave Keon had come from northern Quebec and had been playing with St. Mike's Juniors. Eddie Shack was obtained by way of a trade with the Rangers. Although the Leafs enjoyed their best regular season finish in years, the Red Wings beat Toronto four games to one in the semi-finals.

Before the universal entry draft was established in 1963, the NHL had a system whereby teams discovered talented 16 years of age or older boys and signed them to "C Forms." This then obligated the player to play for that team until he was sold or traded to another team. In order to retain the agreement, the NHL team had to renew the obligation each year on the player's birthday. Once the "C Form" was signed, the player received $100. If the player didn't sign, the team placed the player on their negotiation list anyway. Sponsorship deals were also employed to secure players. NHL teams could claim a player as their own simply by offering financial support to the team on which the player in question played. The Boston Bruins secured Bobby Orr by purchasing his Parry Sound team; the Montreal Canadiens tried to buy the Quebec Aces in order to secure Jean Beliveau, but ended up having to buy the entire Quebec Senior

Hockey League just to get Beliveau signed as a Montreal Canadien.

Dad had heard about David Keon's exceptional skills for a fourteen-year-old player, and flew up to Northern Quebec to see for himself. He discovered an excellent hockey player-and one, which Montreal had under contract. But Stafford wanted Keon so badly that he purchased the entire Rouyn-Noranda team, thus converting Keon's rights over to Toronto. There had always been a sizeable rivalry between the Canadiens and the Maple Leafs, but stealing Dave Keon escalated the animosity between the Montreal Canadiens and Toronto Maple Leafs.

"The Entertainer," Eddie Shack came to the Leafs that year in a trade with New York, and the city of Toronto has never been quite the same since. As for me, Shack has remained a friend through the years. Like only a handful of others, Eddie was one of the Leafs in the sixties to participate in all four Stanley Cup victories. Every time I see him, Eddie laughs that infectious laugh of his and hollers. "Tommy, lemme see your old man's ring." Neither one of us goes a day without wearing that rare four-Cup ring.

After he first arrived in Toronto, Eddie came in to Doug Laurie's Sports where I happened to be working, and introduced himself. We chatted for a lengthy time, and just as he turned to leave, he asked, "Could you introduce me to your dad and your grandfather? I've heard about them for years when I was a kid in Sudbury, and while playing for the Guelph Biltmores in Junior. I'm proud to be a Maple Leaf, and I'd love to shake their hands."

Just about every day, Eddie would pop in to see me in Doug Laurie's. He always made me laugh with one crazy comment or another. It wasn't too long after I first met him that he asked me a favour. His request sounded serious, so we entered the privacy of my tiny office at Doug Laurie's. To be honest, it was once a closet. Eddie and I could barely fit in it together. He really got a kick out of the one-way glass installed in the office. Customers couldn't see in, but I could watch the store and the cash register from my office while I ordered stock or held a close meeting. Eddie began, "Tom, do you know I can't read or write?"

"Eddie," I responded in shock. "I had no idea. How would I know something like that?"

He said, "Well, does it bother you now that you know?" "Not in the slightest," came my response. "In fact, is there some way I can help you out with it?" Eddie looked at me and started to whisper, "If I show you contracts and important things like that, can I trust you to read 'em for me and advise me? And if there are changes that hafta be made, will you tell me? And if the papers are okay, will you let me know before I sign 'em? By the way, about all I can write is my name." I stared back at him. "Eddie," I stated, "I'll help you with anything you want, and I swear that you can trust me. I will keep our conversations private, and I promise that I will be as loyal to you as you are to the Maple Leafs." Many times, Eddie would come in with papers on which he needed advice, and I always helped him the best I possibly could. We still run into each other once or twice a year, and pick up on our conversations as though we see each other every few days.

Although Dad, Punch and just about everybody else in Toronto felt that the 1960-61 season was to be the year of Toronto's return to the Stanley Cup winner's circle, the team fell short. But to say that the management and team were confident about Stanley Cup prospects in 1961-62 would be an understatement. With some minor tinkering, Imlach was going with the team he had methodically pieced together over the previous three seasons. Mahovlich, Keon, Armstrong, Kelly, Nevin, Pulford, Harris, Olmstead, Shack and Stewart at forward; Horton, Stanley, Baun and Brewer on defense and "the China Wall," Johnny Bower in goal. Again, Toronto challenged the Canadiens for top spot all year, but when the final buzzer of the regular season rang, Toronto was a solid second behind Montreal. In the semi-finals, the Leafs brushed past New York, earning a shot at the Stanley Cup against the previous year's champions, the Chicago Blackhawks.

Toronto had home ice advantage in the Stanley Cup finals against the Hawks owing to a higher regular season finish. The Leafs won games one and two in Toronto, but the Hawks fought back with home-ice victories of their own to even the series. Game five, back in Toronto, saw Bob Pulford score a hat trick to lead Toronto to victory. Game six was back to Chicago, where the Hawks had played so well in this series. Punch usually gave great pre-game pep talks, but he let the silence speak volumes before this game. The team knew what it had to do.

After two periods, the score was 0-0 in spite of Toronto outshooting the Hawks 27 to 12. In the third period, the Hawk's star, Bobby Hull, scored to break the deadlock, but Bob Nevin got it back for the Leafs two minutes later. My childhood hero, Dick Duff, scored the Leafs second goal four minutes after that. When the score clock ran down to 00:00, the scoreboard showed the Leafs with two goals, the Hawks with one. The Toronto Maple Leafs had won the Stanley Cup.

The players went crazy, throwing their sticks and gloves sky-ward like schoolchildren at the end of the school year. My Dad and his partners in the Silver Seven embraced like they were welcoming home war heroes. It was all Punch Imlach could do to hold onto his trademark fedora as he hugged everyone. The Chicago crowd gave the Leafs an extremely respectful ovation, and back home, fans spewed out onto Yonge Street in a sponta-neous victory celebration. This was a momentous occasion. The Toronto Maple Leafs had gone from the dregs of the league to hockey supremacy.

The city of Toronto gave the team and management a tickertape parade down Bay Street. Convertibles holding the

Maple Leaf players rolled down Toronto's financial strip, allowing thousands of fans to acknowledge each player. And there in the front of the parade sat Captain George Armstrong, cradling the Cup like a newborn.

When the players disembarked from the caravan in front of City Hall, they looked up in unison to see a wondrous sight at the top of the flagpole: a monstrous blue-and-white flag with the Maple Leaf in the centre.

Chapter Ten

Behind the Scenes

I started my career as a Toronto Maple Leaf employee as a six-year-old stickboy. For a grade-one student, it was a real lesson in focusing. I had to watch the player's sticks on the ice at all times — not watch the play or the crowd or the players on the bench. I also had to memorize all the player's numbers. That's a difficult task for anyone, let alone a six-year-old. Even today, most of the players' names and numbers from my days as a stickboy are still ingrained in memory: #1: Harry Lumley; #2: Jim Thomson; #4: Harry Watson; #7: Max Bentley; #8: Sid Smith; #9: Teeder Kennedy; #11: Howie Meeker; #14: Rudy Migay; #15: Tod Sloan.

My second job with the Maple Leafs was to learn the security system. I was to circle the Gardens during hockey games to make certain the ushers and usherettes were doing their jobs properly. It was their responsibility to help fans find their seats, and to watch for fans with beer, alcohol or cigarettes. Maple Leaf Gardens was a non-drinking facility up until the nineties.

When the referee blew the whistle for a stoppage in play, the ushering staff was to turn around, face the crowd and make sure no fan threw anything onto the ice surface. From time to time, some ushers and usherettes let their allegiance to the Leafs get the best of them, and they spent more time watching the ice. It was these members of the ushering staff who were not doing their jobs properly, and I was to make note.

I recall one time circling the building and going to my dad in his private box to report that everything was okay. Stafford's box was under the balcony in the northeast corner. He looked at me sternly and said, "Tommy, if everything is okay, then tell me why the usher in Section 62 is eating a hot dog?" Frustrated, I immediately went to that section, but by the time I got there, the hot dog was gone. I felt embarrassed that Dad had caught me not doing my job effectively. My dad treated me like an employee, which, in fact I was but if I ever thought I'd catch a break just because I was a Smythe, I was wrong. Dad never missed a trick on the ice or in the stands.

My next professional opportunity with the team was to spend time with Tommy Nayler, the Leaf's assistant trainer and equipment manager. Although I was to learn loads from Tommy, it was anything but a lesson, as he was so much fun and so interesting to watch. I spent as much time as I could with him soaking up every bit of information possible.

I learned all about skates from Tommy Nayler. He had a little room hidden away under the south-end boxes, a short walk to both the Leafs bench and the home dressing room. Up until my time with him, I had no idea that players used more than one pair of skates per season. Each player wore custom-made CCM Tacks (short for Tackaberrys), the highest grade of skate available at the time. But even though they were custom made to each player's specifications, Tommy adjusted them even further to make them exactly right. And I'll never forget his skate-sharpening skills, unequalled to this day. Even players from other teams would ask Tommy for special help when they were in Toronto. Figure skaters from around the world would make a special trip to the city, just to get Tommy to adjust and sharpen their skates. Often, Tommy would suggest changes to CCM, and they would listen to him.

I would watch Tommy sharpen the entire team's skates one by one, reaching behind him, softly filing off the edges and wiping the blade. Then, without looking, he would stand the finished skate beside the one he'd just worked on, which would be balanced and freestanding on its blade. I couldn't believe my eyes: 44 skates, each standing perfectly alone on its blade. Then, with one finger, Tommy would gently nudge the last skate in line so the entire collection would cascade like dominoes. After all the skates were laying down in perfect symmetry, Tommy would say, "Well Tom, there's no sense letting anyone else know our little secret. Let's go to the grill for a snack," and the two of us would head off for a sandwich. He once had a pair of skates made for me, and joked me about my skate size—7 by W4. "No wonder you can't skate worth a damn," he chuckled. Regardless, I never skated so well as I did after I had my custom-made skates from Tommy Nayler.

As I continued my education behind the scenes at the Gardens, I apprenticed with Bob Haggert, who would later become the head trainer of the Maple Leafs. I'd known Bob since I was a young boy, and he was a good friend. Bob had started as a stickboy for the Marlboros and went on to be assistant trainer with them before he moved up to the Maple Leafs. When he joined the Leafs in 1960, he was the youngest head trainer in the NHL. His mother ran the media room, providing sandwiches and soft drinks for the journalists.

Bob taught me all about hockey sticks. He let me watch the players work on their sticks, preparing a model, which the hockey stick manufacturers used to customize, in quantity for each player. Players would make stipulations on how light or heavy they liked their sticks. The angle at which the blade comes off the shaft is called the "lie," and each player had a preference in that area too. A number of players liked a lot of flexibility in the shaft of the stick, but I found the defensemen liked a stronger, sturdier stick. These patterned sticks were just like gold: light, strong with a short life span, but a real bonus for each player.

Bob taught me to watch for a player's pattern getting low and how to order plenty in before the player ran out. Doug Laurie Sports, the sports store which was located in Maple Leaf Gardens and that I later would own, took the stick orders and passed them on to manufacturers like CCM, Hespeler and Northland Pro. Doug Laurie's would also stock the backup supply.

My education continued with Paul Morris. You may not know the name, but you absolutely know the voice. For 38 years, beginning in 1960, Paul was the public address voice for the Toronto Maple Leafs, announcing starting lineups, all the goals, assists, penalties and his famous, "Last minute of play in this period." Paul's voice yielded no emotion, offering absolute objectivity, yet was so distinctive that even now, in retirement, he is being hired to do commercials using his Maple Leaf Gardens style. But Paul was so much more than just a voice. He was also responsible for the sound system at Maple Leaf Gardens. Now, this wasn't just for hockey games — Maple Leaf Gardens has always been used for all sorts of other events, including concerts. Paul taught me about the huge electrical addition at the north end of Maple Leaf Gardens where the Zamboni was kept. This sound system was used for all concerts, with microphones, cords, speakers and huge amplifiers.

As concerts grew to be a bigger part of the Gardens' business, the sound system grew to be more elaborate. With some of the larger acts like Elton John and Rod Stewart, would be a deafening experience. Maple Leaf Gardens became the pre-eminent venue for superstar acts to play in Toronto.

In each city around North America, there is one concert venue that is treasured above all others. In Toronto, that spot was Maple Leaf Gardens. There wasn't an artist or a band that didn't play the Masonic Temple, Massey Hall, the Rockpile, the Horseshoe or the O'Keefe Centre who didn't drive past the Gardens and dream that, one day, they too would play on the stage in that arena.

I was most fortunate to not only have seen most of the greatest performers of all-time perform at the Gardens, but to have gone backstage to meet many of them as well. The very first concert I saw was on April 2, 1957, and it starred Elvis Presley. I was only 11 years old, but remember much of the show, especially the privilege to go backstage afterwards and say hello. It was Elvis's first concert outside of the United States. I saw the Beatles, although I didn't get to meet them. They were amazing, even though I could barely hear them through the screaming.

I met the Dave Clark 5 ("Glad All Over") and enjoyed their concert. In 1965, the Rolling Stones played Maple Leaf Gardens for the first time, and I met them backstage. I've seen one of my favourites, Elton John, play the Gardens four times, but was never fortunate enough to meet him. Meeting and watching Frank Sinatra was an absolute thrill. And who could ever forget the Madonna show? Through the years, I saved all the ticket stubs from every concert, hockey game and special event I attended at the Gardens, and had them arranged inside a huge frame. It makes for a great conversation piece when visitors see it hanging on the wall in my family room.

With all the concerts I've seen, it's hard to pin down which has been my favourite, but I think it had to be Rod Stewart's. I took my daughter Christy and her best friends, Jennifer Addison, and Clair Sturgess. The stage was set up in a "T" formation, and the tickets for the girls were in Row A-amazing seats right by the stage. Towards the end of the show, Rod noticed the 14-

year-old girls gazing at him in awe. He sat down on the edge of the stage, dangled his feet over and sang directly to them. The lyrics were, "I will love you forever," and he sang staring right at my daughter and her friends. They were thrilled. Driving home, they screamed for the duration of the ride. Each girl was convinced that Rod had been singing directly to her. "Did you see how he sang that song just to me?" "No way, he was looking right into my eyes." "Uh uh, he was right in front of me." I could barely hear through the shrieks, but I let them enjoy their evening. To this day, each of the girls argues that Rod Stewart was singing his love song exclusively to her.

My first Maple Leaf Gardens music lesson, so to speak, took place September 5, 1965, and although it was memorable, it was so for all the wrong reasons. On the surface, it should have been an amazing show: the Beach Boys with Sonny and Cher. The Beach Boys were on top of the world, charting song after beach worshipping song. "Surfin' Safari," "Surfin' USA," "Little Deuce Coupe" and "Surfer Girl." This music made up the soundtrack to the early 1960s. With the notable exception of the Beatles, the Beach Boys were the biggest group in the world in 1965.

The man who put the "beach" into the Beach Boys was their drummer, Dennis Wilson. He was the only member who actually surfed, and he loved to customize his car for speed-and second glances from the girls. Dennis was the real heartthrob in the band, and was one of three Wilson brothers in the Beach Boys: oldest brother Brian wrote the songs and played bass. Then Dennis, plus youngest brother Carl was the guitarist. Mike Love, the lead singer, was the Wilson boys' cousin. But it was Dennis who had the wild streak in him. We were soon to find out just how wild he really was.

Dennis had somehow found a motor scooter and taken off from Maple Leaf Gardens for Yorkville. He had heard that it was "the place" for musicians to go while in Toronto. No one could find him and the concert was almost ready to begin with a sold-out crowd anxiously waiting. The opening act, Sonny and Cher, was playing their first-ever concert and had the number-one song in North America at the time, "I Got You Babe." Not long before they were set to go on stage, they were told to double their performance time because no one could find Dennis Wilson, and the Beach Boys wouldn't begin without him. I doubt that Sonny and Cher even knew enough material to double their set. Cher, who was a teenager just like me at the time, was freaking out. I sat back stage with Cher and attempted to console her before she had to perform. Just as they were about to step on stage, Sonny heard that someone had located Dennis. Between Sonny and I, we were able to calm Cher down. Sonny thanked me, then turned and the pair walked out on stage. They put on a fantastic show, and their career subsequently continued to grow. Today, I watch Cher on television and see a confident world-wise woman, but I'll always remember my conversation with a shy, scared and insecure little girl.

Throughout the years, I grew much closer to Harold Ballard. He saw how eager I was to learn every facet of the running of Maple Leaf Gardens, so he taught me everything there was to know about concerts, from booking them to the actual on-stage performance element. At one point in 1970, Harold suggested I try my hand at promoting my own concert at the Gardens. I tried to bring in some of the top acts of the day, but was talked around in circles by the New York agents. They knew that Maple Leaf Gardens was the ultimate place to play in Toronto, but didn't know me, and weren't prepared to trust an unknown promoter with one of their key acts. Finally, one agent gave me a break, and allowed me to book Sly and the Family Stone. I had no idea what an experience this would be. Sly and the Family Stone had enjoyed a lot of success with "I Want to Take You Higher," "Hot Fun in the Summertime," and "Everybody is a Star". They played Ottawa on Saturday night and were scheduled to play the Gardens on Sunday at 1pm.

My first call came at 11 o'clock Sunday morning. "We don't fly. We'll be taking a limousine and we'll get there as soon as we can." Now, Ottawa is about a five-hour drive from Toronto on a good day. If they left at 11, they'd get here by four. What? No way.

On top of this, Harold reminded me that we had wrestling scheduled for seven o'clock that night, and the crew needed two hours to reset the Gardens from a concert venue to a wrestling arena. I was already aging by the hour when the next phone call came. "Look, Tommy, the snow is really bad and we're just at Kingston." They kept phoning from cities marginally closer to Toronto, to tell me how sorry they were. But I don't think they knew how sorry I was.

When the limo finally arrived and the doors opened, I discovered where the band got their name. The smoke nearly knocked me out, and to make matters worse, Sly refused to go on stage until he found his red boots. I was past the breaking point. Throwing up my arms, I went to the box office to see where I stood. Needless to say, my concert career began and ended on the same day.

The Sly and the Family Stone concert went ahead, and the sparse crowd who stayed seemed to enjoy the brief 58-minute performance. As time went on and I repeated this story to my peers, I was to discover that Sly Stone was notorious for either showing up late, or not at all. Whether it was the success going to their heads that made them so irresponsible, or the rumoured drug use that was affecting them, I don't know. But I do know that Sly and the Family Stone fell off the musical radar screen shortly after their Toronto date.

When the fans starting arriving for wrestling that evening, the Gardens staff was still setting up the ring. Harold sent me home and told me I was to see him in his office at nine the next morning. I tossed and turned all night, reliving the day I had just had and anticipating the one I was about to have. Harold and my dad met me the next morning as planned, and told me how much money I had lost. I worked for free for a month to help repay my loss, and at the end of it, Harold took me aside and said kindly, "From here on in Tommy, just work with me."

Chapter Eleven

Scout's Honour

Of all my experiences at Maple Leaf Gardens, it was hockey that made me happiest. Learning the nuances of the hockey business gave me more satisfaction than anything else I've experienced in my professional life. And I don't think I could have had a better teacher than Jim Gregory.

My Dad was the one who discovered Jim Gregory. Stafford had seen Jim out scouting minor hockey players in Toronto's east-end and had noticed how focused he was on the games. After running into him in numerous chilly arenas, Dad approached Jim, and asked if he'd like to scout for the Toronto Maple Leaf organization. "I'd love to, Staff." Jim replied, "But a guy's got to make a living, and scouting isn't going to give me enough money to put food on the table." My Dad then offered him a job at Conn's sand and gravel pit in Caledon to go along with the scouting position. They struck the deal right then and there, and it was the start of not only one of the best business decisions Stafford ever made, but of a great mutual friendship as well.

To this day, I can make Jim laugh by saying just one word: "Firestone." Going back to when my grandfather started C. Smythe For Sand, he had a couple of trucks down in the pit, and was forever having to replace the tires, because the freshly cut gravel would tear them within weeks. Conn finally had enough, and went to visit the Firestone dealer to complain. He wanted Firestone to replace the ripped tires, but the dealer absolutely refused. "Mr. Smythe, with all due respect, the tears have nothing to do with the quality of my tires." The dealer explained. "You can't expect that tires are going to last any length of time when your men are running them over those sharp pieces of gravel. Be reasonable, I can't replace your tires for free."

"Fine," huffed Conn. "Then you've just lost yourself a damned fine customer, and I will never use Firestone tires again." And Conn was true to his word. Ever since, the sand and gravel business has used Goodyear tires exclusively on its trucks. Even on Conn's personal vehicles, and those of the rest of his family, none of us were to use Firestone tires at any cost. But Stafford hadn't told Jim Gregory the story, and when the sand company needed to purchase new tires, Jim went back through the records and saw that they had only purchased from Goodyear through the years. Jim felt that he could get a competitive quote by calling the competition, Firestone. When he called for a quote for Conn Smythe's business, Firestone's president and vice-president couldn't believe their ears. They literally leapt into their cars to deliver the offer in person at the Caledon office. When Dad came in, Jim very proudly announced that he was about to receive a very competitive quote in person from the senior executives at Firestone. Dad went white as the Gardens' ice. "You have got to be kidding me, Jim," Stafford sputtered. "If my old man sees anybody from Firestone on the property, you and I will both be looking for new jobs." The two of them ran out of the office to the highway to intercept the Firestone executives before they rolled into the sand yard. Today, some 90 years since Conn made his vow, I still avoid that brand myself, if only to continue another Smythe tradition.

Jim Gregory used to pick me up after school and take me to a hockey game somewhere in Ontario. Sometimes it would be a Junior A game, but it might just as easily be Junior B or midget hockey. Every game was in a different city and had a different set of teams playing. As time went on, others joined our scouting party. Buck Houle, the manager of the eight Marlboro teams, from peewee to Junior A, usually came along. So did Bob Davidson, the head scout for both the Leafs and the Marlboros.

Bob had been a fierce competitor as a player, and he captained the Stanley Cup-winning Leaf team of 1944-45. Eventually, Gus Bodnar, King Clancy and Punch Imlach joined us. Gus had been the league's rookie of the year in 1943-44 while playing for the Maple Leafs. With the Marlboros, he replaced Buck Houle, and was selected as coach of the year in 1967, the year we all won the Memorial Cup. King had played all-star defense for Toronto in the '30s, later coaching and taking on the assistant general manager's role. Punch, of course, coached and managed the Leafs to Stanley Cup victories in 1961-62, 1962-63, 1963-64 and 1966-67. Can you imagine any student ever having better teachers?

With great care and patience, Jim Gregory taught me everything he knew about hockey. Rule number one took the longest to learn because it defied the way hockey is generally viewed. What I needed to grasp was to concentrate 25 percent of my vision on the puck, while the remaining 75 percent focused on where every player on the ice was situated, play-by-play. It took me a year to fully grasp this ability, but by that time, anyone could ask me where any player was on any particular play, and I'd be able to rhyme off locations. With this skill, figuring out who made a mistake that resulted in a goal was easy. Until my father's death, he'd often quiz me completely out of the blue on where every player was situated for both teams for, say, the Leafs' fourth goal in the second period. I got to be as good as my mentors, and was especially pleased when

King Clancy told me how mastering this concept within a year was very quick, and how proud he was of my ability. This was a skill you couldn't learn from watching television, as the field of vision on TV prohibits seeing the entire playing surface. To pull it off, you literally have to watch hundreds and hundreds of hockey games. And I can assure you, we did.

To learn to be a great scout, you have to watch for very specific talents. Gus Bodnar taught me to watch how players focus on the game, and if they're supporting each other. He knew that without each player assuming his role, teams were certain to wither come playoff time. Bob Davidson taught me to watch for skating, size, focus, strength, shooting, passing, hitting, eyesight and depth of character. Clancy taught me to look for desire. He wanted players who wanted to win at any price. Throughout my entire hockey career, I never met anyone who had as strong a hunger to win every game as King. Jim Gregory taught me everything he knew about the game.

These gentlemen taught me something else, too: poor eating habits. It was exciting and usually humourous to scout with guys like Clancy and Gregory, but we'd often be in some town outside of Toronto late at night and my partners would want to eat. I could never adapt to eating so late. I know this is where I picked up my addiction to Coca-Cola and ice cream. If I wasn't ready for another meal, I'd usually order something, often a banana split. My Mom could never figure out why I seldom wanted breakfast.

On one scouting trip to Rochester, Punch, King and Gregory left Toronto during rush hour. The traffic held them up, so Punch pressed down hard on the accelerator to make the game on time. King always hated the way Punch drove and began to panic when he saw the speedometer pass 70, whip by 80, then hit 90 miles an hour. King threatened to set the car on fire if Punch didn't slow down, but sure enough, the car accelerated to 100 miles an hour. King grabbed a newspaper, rolled it up and lit it on fire in the backseat. Punch couldn't believe his eyes, and screeched to a halt on the shoulder of the highway. Both Imlach and Gregory grabbed handfuls of snow, tossing them on the fire. King idly watched and laughed so hard he could barely breathe. "Will ya slow down now Imlach, or do I have to light it up again?" he snorted. Punch was screaming a blue streak of obscenities at Clancy. Tired with their antics, Gregory shook the car keys in front of both of them and asked, "Do you both want to walk to the game, or are you gonna sit in the car and shut-up 'til we get there?" Astonished, both Clancy and Imlach looked at each other, then glanced at Gregory and yelled, "Who the fuck do you think you are?" to which Jim snidely replied, "I'm the only one with keys to this car." Yes, scouting was a job, but I can assure you we had enormous fun with all the Leafs staff.

There is one scouting story of which I'm especially proud. It's about a player named Bob Dailey. Dailey was a big brawny kid from Kingston, Ontario. At 15 years of age, he stood 6 foot 5, weighed 240 pounds and was playing defense for a team in Belleville. He was tough and focused, but way too slow. In 1970, when it came time for the final draft choice of the day, I couldn't forget Dailey's size and character, and I took him for the Marlboros with pick number 186. My peers howled. The old-timers scouting for the other Junior A teams kidded me that Bob skated like he was wearing snowshoes. The media picked up on the joking. Finally, I had had enough and blurted out, "Look guys. If somebody can work with him on his skating, I know I sure wouldn't want to play against him." Bob Dailey ended up making me look like I owned a crystal ball. He helped the Toronto Marlboros to two consecutive Memorial Cup finals; he was a first-round NHL draft pick, ninth choice overall, for the Vancouver Canucks in 1973, and later went on to play in two NHL all-star games as a member of the Philadelphia Flyers. And all these years later, Bob Dailey is still a close personal, friend.

Chapter Twelve

In This Corner

When you think about Muhammad Ali, it is fighting that immediately comes to mind. But that's only the half of it.

Born Cassius Clay, Ali changed his name to the Islamic Muhammad Ali and renounced his birth-name, stating it was a "slave name." Toronto boxing fans were well aware of his pugilistic prowess, having watched him on closed circuit screens that Maple Leaf Gardens had broadcast. With Ali came a load of trouble. He was a conscientious objector to the Vietnam War. When he refused to be inducted into the U.S. Armed Forces, he was sentenced to five years in jail as a draft dodger; time he never served. Because of his perceived anti-American stance, there wasn't an arena in the United States, which would take Muhammad Ali's scheduled fight against Ernie Terrell. Harold Ballard offered Maple Leaf Gardens for an Ali bout, but it wasn't against Terrell, but rather Canadian heavyweight champion, George Chuvalo. The offer was accepted and the plans were initiated.

Harold had discussed the decision with his partners, John Bassett and my father. After much squabbling Stafford backed down and agreed that he'd allow the fight to proceed. They mutually agreed that the attention drawn to the Gardens would be outstanding, and the profits would certainly be outstanding too. They placed the ticket price at $100 per seat. On the day the match was to be announced, Dad told Conn about it, and it became the most vicious of their thousands of fights. My grandfather did not want a draft dodger in Maple Leaf Gardens, especially considering the war records of both Conn and Stafford. Conn was disgusted, and swore that if the Ali-Chuvalo fight went ahead as planned, he would resign as a director of Maple Leaf Gardens, and never speak to my father again.

I had the opportunity to meet Ali, and we talked for a few minutes. Then I watched him warm up. Ali was punching the bag so fast that it blurred my vision. I couldn't get over how fast his hands could move. When he stopped working over the bag, Ali took off his warm-up gloves, put a piece of masking tape on them and autographed them to me. Of all the momentoes I've collected over the years, these gloves are among my most treasured souvenirs.

Ali and Chuvalo stood toe to toe on the evening of March 29, 1966. With ringside tickets at an inordinately high $100 apiece, the bout wasn't the windfall that Harold, Bassett and my Dad had envisioned. But it was an incredible battle; certainly the greatest ever seen in Maple Leaf Gardens. Ali averaged 75 hits per minute for the first 12 rounds. At the press conference before the fight, Muhammad Ali referred to the Toronto native, Chuvalo, as "an old washerwoman." But that old washerwoman put up one hell of a fight, and after 15 rounds, both boxers were still on their feet and conscious. Many believed that Ali eased up near the end. Although Muhammad Ali was awarded the victory, George Chuvalo did himself and all of Canada proud.

Grandpa's resignation from the board of directors over the boxing match was accepted. The Conn Smythe era at Maple Leaf Gardens was over after 34 incredible years. But the standoff between Dad and Grandpa was just beginning. It tore me apart. I loved them both dearly, and was caught right in the middle. Both were stubborn as mules when they wanted to be. I didn't know if there was anything that I could do to resolve the impasse.

Conn and I were very close from the time I was born until the moment I sat with Grandpa as he drew his final breath. But one night, as we watched the Leafs from his private box together like always, Conn took some unnecessary verbal shots at my Dad. I'd had enough. "Look Grandpa, I enjoy watching the games with you, but if you are going to speak against my Dad, I'll see you next game." This went on game after game, and it took an entire year until Conn and I could sit together for even one period. Another year passed before Grandpa and I could get through two periods without him denigrating my father. It took another year, and we finally made it through a full game together. Conn glanced over and shook my hand. "I know what you've been up to, Tom," he said. "I congratulate you on your patience. If your Dad will apologize, we'll be friends again."

Negotiating with a Smythe is never as easy as it seems. I went to my Mom, and together, we planned how we could get the two of them to drop their feud. Mom and I convinced Dad that Conn would bury the past if Stafford would provide his father with a new lifetime office in the Gardens and a Cadillac. Dorothea designed a fabulous suite, and I arranged the car through my friends Clarke and Harry Addison. When all was ready, I took Conn and Stafford up to Grandpa's new office to cut the ceremonial red tape. The two looked at each other for what seemed like an eternity. They shook hands, smiling broadly, then reached out and hugged each other. It was an emotional moment for all of us. And considering the successes I've been fortunate enough to achieve through my life, bringing my Dad and grandfather back together is probably my greatest accomplishment.

Chapter Thirteen

Centennial Hat Trick

Canada's centennial year was met with extravagant plans for celebration from coast to coast. Every community across the country, it seemed, was involved in its own centennial project. Arenas and community centres sprang up like spring flowers. There wasn't a school in Canada that didn't sponsor its own centennial poetry contest, musical pageant or historical re-creation. Toronto trumpeter, Bobby Gimby, had us all singing, "Ca-na-da, one little, two little, three Canadians..." Families packed their campers and headed for Montreal, the home of Expo 67, the exceptional world exhibition. And the Smythe family commemorated 1967 with its own celebrations.

During 1966-67, I had the honour of being named assistant manager of the Toronto Marlboros, working closely with my friend and mentor Jim Gregory, who was the team's general manager. Harold Ballard, president of the Toronto Marlboro Hockey Club, and my father, Stafford, who was the managing director, announced my appointment. I was only 21 years old, which was extraordinary when you realize that the Marlboro's captain, Brian Glennie, was 20. Don't think for a second that I was spoiled for being born a Smythe, as that was certainly not the case. I simply had a gift for hockey and was given the opportunities to exploit it.

The Toronto Marlboros were solid as a rock my first year as assistant manager. Glennie, who went on to play with the Leafs, was joined by future Hall of Famer Brad Park, Mike Byers, Gerry Meehan, Mike Pelyk and a number of others who went on to play in the National Hockey League or the World Hockey Association. Our goalie was Gary Edwards, who enjoyed a lengthy career in the NHL. We beat the Montreal Junior Canadiens and the Hamilton Red Wings to earn our shot at the Quebec Junior Hockey League's Thetford Mines Canadiens. Thetford Mines boasted future NHLers Gilbert Perreault, Marc Tardif and Rejean Houle, but the Marlboros defeated them, too. We had made it to the Memorial Cup final, and would be facing the Port Arthur Marrs.

All the games were to be played at the Fort William Gardens in Thunder Bay, Ontario. Toronto played unbelievable hockey. We were all over the Marrs, and took the 1966-67 Memorial Cup in five games. This was the fifth Memorial Cup for the Toronto Marlboro franchise, and as assistant manager, I was proud to have played a significant role in our victory.

A major celebration was planned for the next evening in the Hot Stove Club at Maple Leaf Gardens. This was a private members club often used for celebrations of this sort. But I had a problem — I needed a date. Because I had been so focused on hockey, I hadn't taken a girl out in a long time, and this celebration called for someone special on short notice. After much deliberation, I remembered a girl I had met at the very first Harvey's hamburger location, on Avenue Road in Toronto. I had only spoken to her for a few minutes and had never been out with her. In fact, I really had no idea how I was going to talk her into going out with me. But somehow, after much conversation I was able to convince Anne to go to the Marlboro Memorial Cup celebration party with me. Who could ever have predicted that this auspicious beginning would lead to Anne becoming my first wife and the mother to our amazing children, Tommy and Christy?

The party ended up being one of the wildest celebrations I have ever experienced. The Marlboros had pushed for this victory all season, and they weren't about to let the evening slip away without celebrating it to the highest degree. For most of the Marlboro players and their dates, the very first taste of champagne they ever had came from the bowl of the Memorial Cup. The party got wilder and wilder, and the bar and bartenders were stretched to their maximum capacity. Thankfully most of the player's parents were there and able to drag their boys home, maybe a little worse for wear, but happier than they'd ever been.

After the Toronto Maple Leafs won the Stanley Cup in 1961-62, talk of "dynasty" filled the sports pages. The 1962-63 season saw the Leafs dominate the regular season, finish in first place and decisively defeat both the Canadiens and the Red Wings to win a second straight Stanley Cup. The team was almost exactly the same as the previous season, with Mahovlich, Keon, Horton and Bower once again leading the way.

The following season, 1963-64, was a more challenging year. Toronto struggled at times through the season, and during the run for the playoffs, Imlach felt he needed to add some scoring punch. The Leafs sent Dick Duff, former Marlboro Bob Nevin and prospects Arnie Brown, Rod Seiling and Bill Collins to the New York Rangers for perennial all-stars Andy Bathgate and Don McKenney. The trade seemed to give Toronto a surge, and when the regular season was completed, the Leafs had finished in third place. Meeting first place Montreal in the semi-finals was a daunting task, but in a hard fought, seven-game series, the Maple Leafs defeated the Habs. The finals paired Toronto against Detroit. Again it went to seven games and, in a taxing battle, the Toronto Maple Leafs defeated the Red Wings, earning their third straight Stanley Cup.

Late in the third period of game six, Leafs' Bob Baun blocked a Red Wing's slap shot shattering his foot instantly. Baun was carried off the ice with multiple factures in his foot, only to return for the beginning of overtime. During intermission Baun demanded that his foot be frozen with local anesthetic injections and at 1:43 of the first overtime period, Baun stepped onto the ice and scored the winning goal to force a seventh and deciding game in the Stanley Cup finals. Bob Baun's selfless bravery exemplified the spirit of the Toronto Maple Leaf organization.

But this was 1967, and the Leafs fortunes had fallen since their last Cup win in 1964. In the two previous seasons, Toronto was knocked out of playoff competition in the semi-finals. The Maple Leafs were becoming an old team. Much of the core group constructed in the late fifties was still there: Mahovlich, Pulford, Armstrong, Horton, Baun and Bower. The early 1960s additions, too, were still with Toronto: Kelly, Keon, Shack and Stanley. But new faces to the Leafs included aging veterans Marcel Pronovost, Terry Sawchuk and Bruce Gamble, as well as youngsters Peter Stemkowski, Jim Pappin, Mike Walton, Brian Conacher and Ron Ellis, all whom had come up through the Leafs farm system.

My jaw still hurts when I recall Ronny Ellis's welcome to the NHL. He lined up for the opening face-off against the Wings' Gordie Howe. Howe asked, "Kid, ya gonna win rookie of the year?" Ellis answered, "Geez, I hope so." Gordie said, "Good luck." Then, just as the puck was dropped, the infamous Howe elbow flew up and caught Ron smack in his mouth. He landed flat on his back, out cold and minus some front teeth. As Ellis groggily came to, Gordie leaned down and whispered, "Welcome to the NHL."

No one truly expected the Toronto Maple Leafs to compete for the Stanley Cup in Canada's centennial year. The Chicago Blackhawks had run away from the pack, finishing a dominant season in first place, 17 points ahead of Montreal. The Leafs completed the season in third place, and would face the Blackhawks in the first round of the playoffs. The contests were tough, but no tougher than the Leaf goaltenders. Bower and Sawchuk were able to stop just about everything snipers Bobby Hull, Stan Mikita and Phil Esposito could fire at them. When the series ended, the Leafs had defeated the Hawks four games to two. The series victory entitled Toronto to a shot at the Cup, but the Montreal Canadiens were not going to be pushovers. I remember thinking how appropriate it was that the NHL's two Canadian teams were facing each other for the Stanley Cup in Canada's centennial year. The Montreal journalists felt it was the Canadiens' divine right to win the Cup, considering Expo 67 was in Quebec. But the Leaf team had a few thoughts on that subject themselves.

The Canadiens took the first game in Montreal. Bower came up huge in game two, stoning Montreal 3-0 in their home rink. Back to Toronto for game three, and Bob Pulford scored in overtime to give the Leafs a victory. Montreal stormed back two days later with a decisive win. The series went back to Montreal for game five; the series deadlocked at two games apiece. The Maple Leafs pulled out all the stops, and beat Montreal to take a three-to-two edge in the series. Then it was back to Toronto for game number six.

"With just over a minute to play, Toronto is leading Montreal two to one. The Canadiens are trying to force a face-off in the Leafs zone, and with that whistle, they'll get it. Toe Blake has called Worsley over to the bench, so the Canadiens will have an extra attacker on the ice for this all-important face-off to the left of Terry Sawchuk. Fifty-five seconds left in regulation time. Oh my. Punch Imlach has defence-man Allan Stanley taking the face-off against Beliveau. The puck is dropped. Stanley ties up Beliveau in the face-off circle, and Kelly swoops in to grab the puck. He dishes it off to Pulford at the Leafs blueline. Pulford cuts across the ice and produces a perfect backhand over to Armstrong, who's skating up the right wing. The captain fires from outside the blueline — scores! Armstrong, into an open net. The Leafs are up three to one and the Canadiens won't come back in this one."

The date was May 2, 1967, and the Toronto Maple Leafs had won the Stanley Cup; their fourth of the decade; the eleventh in franchise history. The Conn Smythe Trophy, presented to the outstanding player of the Stanley Cup playoffs, went to the Toronto Maple Leafs' sensational Davey Keon.

The Stanley Cup party was held at my parents' new home on Ashley Park in Etobicoke. This new house was much larger than the old one, spanning thousands of square feet of living space on a rare two-acre parcel of land. Some 600 people showed up to celebrate the fourth Stanley Cup victory under the Stafford Smythe / Harold Ballard regime. The invitees included every Leaf player, his wife and family, all the Gardens employees and their families — anyone with even a semblance of affiliation to the Toronto Maple Leafs or Maple Leaf Gardens was at the celebration. I had even hired a rock band to keep the party going well into the night. The band was great, but boy, were they loud. The neighbours must have been cursing those Smythes. Come to think of it, I'm pretty sure the neighbours were all at our party too.

Two of the guys in the band were my buddies from Upper Canada College. I had known Rick Bell for years. His father was a pianist with the Toronto Symphony Orchestra, and Rick could play as well as his Dad. But he loved rock and roll far more. Rick joined Ronnie Hawkins and the Hawks, played with Crowbar ("Oh What a Feeling") and eventually joined Janis Joplin's last band, Full Tilt Boogie.

"Monk" Marr was a great musician, and one of the funniest characters I've ever known. He is remembered for pulling crazy stunts in high school. His finest moment had to be the day he disrupted a school assembly. The students were in Mission Hall, with the principal and masters all dressed in black robes. The procession was scheduled to include the Music Master on the huge organ with its beautiful pipes. Once the music processional began, the masters would strut up to the Rector, where the Master Principal would wave us to our seats. Monk had the crazy idea that he was going to pour great quantities of flour into the organ pipes during the night before. Well, the moment came. The Principal nodded his head to the Music Master who, with a flourish, hit the organ keys with all ten fingers and the pedals with both feet. All we heard was an awful belch from the organ pipes, then turned to see a giant cloud of pure white flour descending rapidly on the auditorium! The Masters, once dressed in black from head to foot, were now awash in white flour! The Principal demanded to know the culprit who had perpetrated such an indignity. Ten minutes later, no one had budged. The Principal then demanded that anyone who knew who had caused such a furor to stand up. Still, no one stepped forward. This was a true test of loyalty, as better than half the auditorium knew the answer, but wouldn't give in. The Masters, furious, left the Hall one by one for the showers, returning in clean attire. The student body sat all day; no food, no water or washroom breaks. Every hour, the Principal would ask for the culprit to come forward, and each hour, no response was generated. Finally, at 5:30, a parking lot full of angry parents arranged our release.

Everyone danced and partied well into the night, laughing and embracing and enjoying the fruits of the Stanley Cup victory. Clothing started to come off piece by piece too, although I'll never divulge how far that went or by whom. And as the sun started to peek over the horizon, I looked around to see revelers asleep on the chesterfields, on the floor or anywhere they could find a comfortable spot. My dear Mom spent the entire day and the one following, cleaning up the disaster area. Our new home had certainly been initiated properly.

So, 1967 wasn't quite six months old and already I had won the Memorial Cup with the Toronto Marlboros and Dad had won the Stanley Cup with the Toronto Maple Leafs. We put a ton of good-natured pressure on my grandfather to hold up his end of the winning Smythe tradition. His opportunity was June

24 at Woodbine Racetrack, where the high profile Queen's Plate, a horse race for three year olds, was being held.

My grandmother, Irene, saw one of Conn's fillies shortly after its birth and exclaimed, Isn't she lovely? Grandpa looked at Irene, then down at the filly and decided that the horse's name would be Damned Lovely. Unfortunately for Conn, the commission refused to allow Damned, so the filly became Jammed Lovely. Before Jammed Lovely was old enough to compete in the Queen's Plate, my grandmother died of cancer. Conn and Irene had been married for 45 years.

Conn, like much of the Smythe family, relied on vibes to help guide decisions. Just before the Queen's Plate, Grandpa felt the vibes from Irene. Even though only one filly had ever won the Queen's Plate that century, he felt a hunch from Irene, and entered Jammed Lovely into the competition. Jim Fitzsimmons was jockey for most of Conn's horses at that time, but had been offered the opportunity to ride the race favourite, Betemight. Grandpa told him he was free to choose whichever horse he wished to ride, nevertheless, Jim chose Jammed Lovely. Why Fitz went with a long shot when he had a chance to ride the potential winner, none of us knew, but I can only assume he felt some sort of vibe as well.

World famous jockeys Ron Turcotte and Avelino Gomez came in to ride the two race favourites: Betemight and Pine Point. Jammed Lovely ran very well, but down the stretch was in fourth. Then, Fitz cut Jammed Lovely around one horse then cut her back to the rail where she squeezed into the lead. We were all frantic as Gomez charged for the lead on Pine Point, but Fitz got one more spurt of energy out of Jammed Lovely and she edged Pine Point by a neck. We had won! And the Smythe family had pulled off their hat trick!

The family was overwhelmed with happiness, and we couldn't help but think of Irene. Conn took my sister and two cousins to the winning circle in tribute to my grandmother. The three girls carried the blood and spirit of my grandmother inside them, and that thought comforted Conn a great deal. My grandfather didn't stay in the club celebrating for long. He told everyone to follow him down to the barn, where Grandpa threw a huge party with the jockeys, trainers, stable help and friends and family. It was a great party, and we went through over twenty-eight cases of champagne. I took a rare drink of champagne, looked up to the sky and whispering thank you Irene.

I've only consumed alcohol eight times in my life and each time was but a sip of champagne. But each occasion had major significance in my life. There have been my two weddings, four Stanley Cup victories, a Memorial Cup celebration and the Queen's Plate party that completed the Smythe family hat trick!

Chapter Fourteen

Marlboro Men

Running a Major Junior A franchise is a constant evolution. The best players are lost to the NHL draft each year, so constant scouting and evaluation are necessary to find new recruits and determine the development of current players. The Memorial Cup victory was behind us, and I had taken a year's hiatus to attend Boston University. Upon my return in 1968-69, I was placed in charge of the Toronto Marlboros as the general manager. Slowly and deliberately, I made trades and draft choices, and moved Marlboro players up through the ranks. But while I was constantly manipulating the Marlboro lineup in search of success, I was working very hard at another important project.

I felt very strongly that helmets should be mandatory for Ontario Hockey Association players. Three years before, Dad, Jim Gregory and I had developed the idea. The target was originally NHL players but whenever the NHL owners discussed the subject with them, they received little co-operation. We realized that the only way to make progress in this area was to go through junior hockey. We felt that if helmets were made mandatory at a junior level, these players would continue wearing head protection when they graduated to professional ranks. Eventually, all NHL players would be wearing helmets.

I made it my mandate to get this legislation through for the good of the players. Dad helped me prepare what I would say in the OHA meetings. After two daylong meetings, and more arguments than I care to remember, the owners accepted my proposal, one by one. Helmets became mandatory in the OHA. My Marlboro players grumbled for years, and some of them discarded their helmets the second they joined the NHL. But the players eventually accepted the rule and realized its protection value. The NHL took years to follow suit, but finally did. And with the retirement of Craig MacTavish after the 1996-97 season, the last non-helmeted player had skated in the NHL. We all strive to make a difference, and this is one area, which I consider my small legacy to hockey.

I had found that the parents of teenage athletes quite often caused problems in the running of the team. As a result, there were two other rules I instituted as general manager of the Toronto Marlboros. One was that no parent could sit in on contract negotiations with their children. At the junior level, we're not talking huge deals, but the players were given an honourarium as well as food money and a room-and-board budget. It was surprising that many parents tried to treat junior hockey as though it was the NHL. The other rule I had was that no parents could sit behind the team bench. We welcomed and encouraged parents to attend all games, but they had to sit on the opposite side of the arena. Too often, we had parents chastising the coaches or "suggesting" strategy from behind the bench.

The Marlies were a close-knit group, and of the '60s and '70s alumni, many of the players continue to maintain a friendship, including forwards Glenn Goldup, Steve Shutt, Bill Harris and Dave Gardner, as well as defensemen Mike Amodeo, Steve Durbano and the draft choice they laughed at, Bob Dailey.

Glenn Goldup was all heart. He maximized the use of every part of his body to get the job done. Like me, Glenn had started

Conn Smythe, centre — age 6 with grandfather Albert and father Joseph — 1901 *– credit author collection*

Conn Smythe age 4
— credit author collection

Stafford Smythe age 4
— credit author collection

Irene Smythe
— credit author collection

Major Conn Smythe
— credit author collection

Opening night at the Gardens — 1932 — Boston vs. Toronto —
48th Highlanders performing at centre ice
— credit Imperial Oil – Turofsky – Hockey Hall of Fame

Maple Leaf Gardens. Home of the Toronto Maple Leafs from 1931-1999 60 Carlton Street, Toronto, Ontario, Canada
— credit Imperial Oil – Turofsky – Hockey Hall of Fame

Hugh Smythe, Conn Smythe and Stafford Smythe — Maple Leaf Gardens — 1934
— credit author collection

Maple Leaf great Dick Duff — 1956
— credit author collection

Maple Leaf's Bob Baun fights Ranger's Eddie Shack for the puck, while Leafs' goalie Johnny Bower guards his post– 1958
— credit Graphic Artists Hockey Hall of Fame

Harold Ballard and Red Kelly celebrating the Maple Leafs 1963 Stanley Cup victory *— credit Graphic Artists – Hockey Hall of Fame*

Stafford Smythe and Harold Ballard inspecting Maple Leaf Garden's Hot Stove Lounge — 1963 *— credit Graphic Artists – Hockey Hall of Fame*

Smythe Family, Caledon, Ontario — 1959
Mary, Dorthea, Stafford, Elizabeth, Vicki, Duke the Doug and Tom

Islington Hornets and Islington Redmen Humber Valley Hockey Association 1954. TOP: Bryant Smith, Dave Shaw, Bob Bryant, Ken Dryden, John Harris, Dick Falconer, Mike Evans, John Leetham, Andy Clements, Jack Cambridge. MIDDLE: Bill Sanagan, John Stafford, John Pennal, Bill Cansfield, Dick Edwards, Tom Smythe, Gord Hicks, Pete Legault BOTTOM: Bruce Sinclair, Al Picard, Pete Taylor, John Forsythe, Dave Webb, Doug McCorkingdale, Doug Smith

Stafford Smythe (back row) with son Tommy (centre front) teammates, John Stafford and John Pennal, Humber Valley Hockey Association — Etobicoke — 1954 *— credit author collection*

Maple Leafs trainer Joe Sgro sews the 'C' on Dave Keon's sweater — 1969 *— credit Graphic Artists – Hockey Hall of Fame*

Tommy Smythe, Mary Smythe, Stafford Smythe and Elizabeth Smythe, Maple Leaf Gardens — 1966 – *credit author collection*

Upper Canada College — Toronto — 1963
Brad Chapple, Tommy Smythe, Brian Love and Tom Radford

Rose Kennedy, Stafford Smythe and Harry "Red" Foster
Variety Village — 1962

Jockey — Sandy Hawley, Conn Smythe and Bobby Orr attending a '60s Conn Smythe Dinner — *credit author collection*

Smythe 1967 Centennial Hat Trick

TOP: Stafford Smythe with Stanley Cup — Bay Street Parade — Toronto

MIDDLE Memorial Cup winning Toronto Marlboros

Conn Smythe at Woodbine Race Track — winning the Queensplate

Tom Smythe (centre) with Toronto Marlboros
Maple Leaf Gardens 1970

Glen Goldup, Tommy Smythe, Marty Howe and Dave Gardner
Toronto Marlboros Hockey Club

Maple Leaf Hall of Famer, Frank Mahovlich aboard Stafford Smythe's 32ft Minett (the Big M) Muskoka Antique Boat Show, Port Carling, Muskoka — 1974
— credit auhor collection

Conn Smythe at home 68 Baby Point Road, Toronto — 1978
— credit author collection

Four generations of Smythe men — Conn Smythe, Tom Smythe, Stafford Smythe and (centre) Tom's newborn son Tommy. Maple Leaf's dressing room — 1971
— credit author collection

Stafford Smythe with grandson Tommy and daughter Elizabeth — Maple Leaf Gardens — 1971
— credit author collection

Conn with Jammed Lucky — Caledon, Ontario

Smythe Family Christmas — 1986 — BR: Don Mathison, Conn Smythe Jr., Tom Smythe, Dr. Hugh Smythe, Elizabeth Brinton, Robbie Swatuck, Vicky Scarlett, Sarah Scarlett, Tommy Smythe, Dorthea Smythe, Bernice Smythe. FR: third from left, Christy Smythe, bottom right, Anne Smythe

Harry Addison with daughter Jennifer, Christy Smythe and father Tom — Father/ Daughter Ball, Branksome Hall — Toronto —1987

Leaf Hall of famers, George Armstrong, Bob Pulford and Ted Kennedy, along with Tom Smythe, present the J.P. Pickell award to Bob Davidson for his lifetime contribution to the Leafs — Maple Leaf Gardens — 1995

Maple Leafs current owner, Steve Stavro presents Tom Smythe with Maple Leaf Alumni pin — Director's Room — Maple Leaf Gardens — 1995

Penny Brown, Tom, Christy & Tommy Smythe in Maple Leafs Directors' room — closing night of MLG — February 13th — 1999

Closing night ceremonies at Maple Leaf Gardens February 13th —1999

Toronto Maple Leafs new home — Air Canada Centre.
Bay Street, Toronto — 2000.

his hockey career in the Humber Valley Hockey Association as a seven-year-old. He later joined the Toronto Marlboro organization as a peewee. Glenn is the son of Hank Goldup, who won a Stanley Cup with the Leafs in 1941-42, and later played with the Rangers. Although not skilled enough to be a first-line player, Glenn showed focus and loyalty beyond the call of duty, and improved with each season. He did eventually achieve his dream and played in the NHL, first as a reserve with Montreal, later with the Los Angeles Kings.

Back when he was a Marlie, Glenn would do odd jobs for me during the summers. One day, I rented a truck to move appliances and furniture to our family's cottage on Lake Joseph in Ontario's Muskoka cottage country. Bruce O'Niel from Doug Laurie's sports store was also there to help. The first half of the trip was no problem — trudge down the steep hill to the cottage, unload the goods, hook up the appliances. We then grabbed some lunch, did some water-skiing and swimming. The day was beautiful. But when it came time to head back to Toronto, Glenn couldn't turn the truck around, and we realized that it now had to be backed up the steep hill and all the way out the quarter-mile driveway. Glenn jumped behind the wheel and told me to guide him. The tires screamed and the rubber burned as Glenn backed the truck up the hill. I steered him around trees and corners until I heard an awful scream. It was Bruce. Rushing around to the other side of the truck, I heard Glenn shouting and howling with laughter. "What the hell do I do now, Tom? I got the bastard pinned between the truck and the tree?" Glenn attempted to keep the truck from rolling back down the hill and inadvertently pinned Bruce even tighter. Slowly-very slowly, Glenn inched the truck away, and within a minute, Bruce was freed. It could have been much worse, but Bruce managed to brush himself off, marked with only minor abrasions. We continued the trip, returned the truck and had a new tale to tell. Glenn Goldup still runs the Toronto Marlboro Alumni

Golf Tournament in Bolton, Ontario each year. I usually go, if for no other reason than to drive the golfcarts for some of my dearest friends and to keep Glen from getting behind the wheel.

Steve Shutt and Bill Harris were the superstars of those Marlboro teams. They hold several records and were the heart and soul of those teams. It took me a long time to find an appropriate centre to play with them. Harris and Shutt were fast, and were real snipers who needed someone who could not only keep up with them, but who could get them the puck. After many conversations with Dave Gardner, and some very tough talks with his dad, former Maple Leaf Cal Gardner, I was able to convince Dave to leave St. Michael's where he was playing Junior B, to join the Toronto Marlboros. Naysayers felt Gardner was too thin, and he was, but we worked hard at adding both weight and strength. But what attracted me to Dave were his speed and his vision-both quick as lasers. Dave Gardner completed the final piece to the dream line puzzle. The three combined for 342 points during the 1970-71 season, and 370 in 71-72, still a Major Junior A record. But as fast as they were on the ice, they were, like Goldup, equally fast off the ice.

One night, we were on an overnight trip to Montreal for a very pivotal game. Harris and Shutt were sharing a room, and had it stacked from floor to ceiling with cases of beer. The entire team worked diligently to ensure that I didn't discover their party supplies. I called a short team meeting.

"All right boys, tomorrow we've got a big game and we've got to be ready. You're on your own tonight, but tomorrow morning at nine, we're on the ice for a full equipment practice. Get your sleep and I'll see you tomorrow bright and early." Well, I gave them their wake-up calls and the entire team was a mess. The practice was awful and the boys were really suffering. Most of them went straight back to their hotel rooms after practice and slept until it was time to report for the game. I'd never have believed that they'd be ready to play, but the team performed well and we won, and my first line performed brilliantly. On the train ride home, the team tried to convince me that the beer was responsible for our victory. Dave Gardner debuted in the NHL as a Montreal Canadien, later playing for St. Louis, the old California Golden Seals and the Cleveland Barons. He capped off his career with the Flyers. Bill Harris went on to star with the New York Islanders, and later played with both L.A. and Toronto. Steve Shutt played 13 exceptional years with the Montreal Canadiens, finishing his career with the Kings, and receiving hockey's highest honour — an inclusion in the Hockey Hall of Fame in 1993.

Another Marlie Mike Amodeo, was a very tough but exceptionally quiet defenseman. Mike first played professionally in the World Hockey Association with the Toronto Toros, then later with the Winnipeg Jets. When Winnipeg joined the NHL, Mike came with the team. Steve Durbano earned his NHL stripes with St. Louis, Pittsburgh and the Kansas City Scouts, moving with them to Colorado when the franchise was relocated. He also played a year in the WHA with Birmingham.

One of the most exciting moments in my hockey career was securing Marty and Mark Howe for the Toronto Marlboros. The sons of NHL legend Gordie Howe, the boys had been incredible on Detroit-area travel teams. I knew that I was in competition with virtually every university in North America and every league in the world for the services of Marty and Mark. But I had learned my lessons well, and I focused all my energies on obtaining the Howe brothers. There were many trips down Highway 401 between Toronto and Windsor to visit Gordie and Colleen Howe at their home in Detroit. But I offered something that no one else had, and that was Maple Leaf Gardens — home to the spirit of both Memorial Cups and Stanley Cups. There is an aura about Maple Leaf Gardens that fascinates fans, and the Howes were no different. On Canada Day, 1970, I had my own celebration when Gordie Howe called my parents' cottage in

Muskoka to tell me that Marty would join the Marlboros for the 1971-72 season, and that Mark would follow a year later. I was so excited, that I could barely stammer out a "thank you." My dad was more excited than I had ever seen him, and gave me a monstrous bear hug. Stafford was never as proud of me, before or after, as he was when I got off the phone from Gordie Howe that incredible day.

Chapter Fifteen

Expansion

The hockey world changed following the 1966-67 season. Expansion introduced six new teams to the NHL in time for the 1967-68 season. New to the league were the Los Angeles Kings, Minnesota North Stars, Oakland Seals, Philadelphia Flyers, Pittsburgh Penguins and St. Louis Blues. Toronto like all "Original Six" franchises lost many very solid hockey players, and some prospects designated as "can't miss." Among them were: goaltenders Terry Sawchuk (Los Angeles) and Gary Smith (Oakland); forwards Eddie Shack (Los Angeles), Gerry Ehman (Oakland) and Brit Selby (St. Louis); as well as defensemen Kent Douglas (Oakland), Bob Baun (Oakland), Larry Hillman (Minnesota) and Al Arbour (St. Louis). Red Kelly went to the L.A. Kings to coach.

Around the same time, Toronto sold its two main farm teams. The Rochester Americans had won the Calder Cup as American Hockey League champions in 1965-66. The Americans featured many players who made the trip up to the Leafs, including Jim Pappin, Larry Jeffrey, Mike Walton, Gerry Ehman, Brian Conacher, Ed Litzenberger and Bronco Horvath. One of the assistant captains was television personality Don Cherry. The Victoria Maple Leafs were also champions in 1965-66, but for

Victoria, it was the Lester Patrick Trophy as winners of the Western Hockey League. Familiar names included Aut Erickson, Andy Hebenton, Milan Marcetta and Larry Keenan.

The Toronto Maple Leafs had been decimated by expansion and the loss of so much young talent from the sale of their farm teams. After the nirvana of sipping champagne from the Stanley Cup, the Leafs tumbled to fifth place in 1967-68, and they missed the playoffs entirely. They have yet to win the Stanley Cup again.

Stafford worked hard on NHL expansion in tandem with the other team owners. But Alan Eagleson, a Toronto lawyer, often thwarted him and the owners. Eagleson had been around the Gardens for several years, doing business with many of the Leafs. He had known Bob Pulford from the time they were teenagers, and Pulford brought Eagleson into the Leafs inner sanctum. In 1960, Bob Baun, Carl Brewer, Billy Harris and Bob Pulford formed a partnership with Eagleson and another young lawyer named Bob Watson. They called their association the Blue and White Investment Group, and together they invested in the stock market. Each partner contributed $1,000 to start, followed by $50 each month. The group made a handsome profit on their investment over the course of several years.

Alan Eagleson began his work as a player representative by perusing Bob Pulford's contracts and offering advice. One of his first clients was Carl Brewer; another was Mike Walton, then in June 1967, Alan Eagleson announced that the National Hockey League Players Association had been formed. Player representatives from the original six NHL clubs met in Toronto to espouse a foundation and elect its president. The representatives were Boston's Ed Johnston, Chicago's Pierre Pilote, Detroit's Norm Ullman, Montreal's Bobby Rousseau and J.C. Tremblay, New York's Rod Gilbert, Harry Howell and Bob Nevin, and Toronto's Bob Pulford.

The NHLPA was created as a player's labor union with a mandate to represent and defend their interests. At the initial meeting, newly elected president Bob Pulford informed team owners that their refusal to accept the new association meant the players would seek recognition through the Canadian Labour Relations Board. The players further wanted a guarantee that being a member of the NHLPA would not expose them to ill treatment by their teams, or the league. The owners agreed. And in return, the NHLPA acceded that the players would not strike for the duration of the agreement, so long as the owners did not breach any terms or conditions.

The players appointed Alan Eagleson as the first Executive Director of the NHLPA. He held the position until the end of 1991, when the players elected to replace him with Robert Goodenow. The call for change by the players stemmed from suspicions of Eagleson's criminal activity within the association. Carl Brewer, one of Eagleson's first clients was one of the key players involved in helping unraveling his fiefdom. The Law Society of Upper Canada, Hockey Canada, the RCMP, the FBI and a Massachusetts grand jury all gathered evidence on Eagleson and on January 6, 1998, Eagleson plead guilty in a Boston court to three counts of fraud. He agreed to pay a set fine of $1,000,000CDN. That same year, Eagleson pleaded guilty to additional fraud charges in a Toronto court and was sentenced to 18 months in jail. In shame, Eagleson withdrew his spot in the Builders category of the Hockey Hall of Fame.

Problems between my dad and Eagleson grew steadily. My father could see how outrageous Eagleson's contract demands were, and he tried to alert the other owners to the depth of Eagleson's greed, both for the future of the NHL and for its players. To me, it has always been sad that Stafford did not live long enough to see how dangerous Eagleson became to the entire NHL. Indeed, the widespread introduction of player agents for contract negotiations — and the explosion of salaries that resulted — rendered the NHL totally changed. Hockey has never been quite the same.

After their respective Stanley Cup and Memorial Cup victories, The Leafs and the Marlboros were forced into rebuilding phases. Hours after the Boston Bruins knocked the Leafs out of the playoffs in four straight games during the spring of 1969, my dad fired Punch Imlach, moving John McLellan in to coach and making Jim Gregory the general manager. Both had been working for the Tulsa Oilers, the Leafs Central Hockey League farm team. Prior to a year off to attend Boston University, I had been assistant manager of the Marlies under Jim Gregory. I then returned to the Marlboros, this time as assistant manager to my old scouting pal Buck Houle. After a year with Houle, I was made general manager of the Toronto Marlboros. It was 1970.

Slowly, the team became stronger on the ice, and was closer than ever off the ice. Little touches made an incredible difference. I took the entire team to A. Winestock's Clothing for Men, an upscale Toronto men's clothing store, where each player was fitted with grey flannel slacks and a double-breasted sports jacket in Marlboro dark blue with a Marlboro crest on the breast pocket. The guys looked great, and the mandatory dress attire gave the Marlboros a really smart appearance. Even the Maple Leafs took notice. They teased Jim, "Hey Gregory, where the hell are ours?"

Since the inception of the Marlboros, the team had been graced with so many notable players who went on to great success in the NHL. During my tenure with the team, it was no different. I recall so many young, eager and excited players donning the Marlboro blue and dreaming of a career with a NHL franchise.

Steve Durbano had joined the Marlboros for the 1968-69 season. From the minute I saw him, I knew that I was glad he was on our side. He contributed just 11 points, but his penalty minute total was 158. In 1969-70, Steve earned 32 points, but had a monstrous total of 371 penalty minutes-more than double any other Marlboro player. The next season, his last as a Marlie, Durbano scored 39 points, but his penalty total remained astronomical-324 penalty minutes for the season. In 1970, Steve Durbano had a running feud going with one of the St. Catharines Blackhawk's defensemen.

One night in St. Catharines, Durbano flattened the player at centre ice during warm-up. This instigated a free-for-all and every player on both teams dropped their gloves and paired off. There were no referees or linesmen on the ice — they were still in their dressing rooms. The coaches hadn't even stepped out from the dressing rooms yet either. The police and some fans jumped onto the ice to try to break up the melee. Someone hollered to us, "Get out to the ice — your players are going wild!" With the Marlboro coach, Frank Bonello, I raced out to ice level and couldn't believe my eyes. We yelled at the players to break it up, and I grabbed Durbano and pulled him towards the dressing room. A policeman started to bark at Durbano, not like an authority figure, but like a crazed hockey fan. Steve didn't take too kindly to that, and lunged at the cop, pulling his hat down over his head then pushing him out the back doors of the rink, into the snow shavings left by the Zamboni. In the midst of all this, the cop's badge cut his forehead. So it was down to the police station for Steve Durbano. I went with him, hoping to get Durbano released. While I was inside chatting up the police lieutenant, the game played on, and the team bus pulled up for us outside the station. Finally, they let Steve go — reluctantly. That entire two-hour bus trip was chatter and bravado all the highway home.

Another night in Ottawa, Gavin Kirk, one of our more offensive Marlboro forwards, was crowding the crease, and an Ottawa 67's defensemen brought his stick up and took the end of Gavin's nose off. There was blood everywhere, and the medical staff, some of the Marlies and I helped load Gavin into the ambulance. I told Frank Bonello that I'd ride with Gavin to the hospital and stay with him in Ottawa if need be. As the back doors of the ambulance closed, tough guy Durbano came running down the sidewalk in his skates, yelling at us. "Wait, wait. Ya gotta take this!" and he handed me a small cup of ice. "What's this?" I asked. Durbano replied, "It's the end of Gavin's nose packed in ice." Stunned, I grabbed the cup. Durbano continued: "I told that goddamn 67 defensemen I'd take his entire fucking nose off if I saw his skates back on this ice surface again tonight." He laughed and returned to the game, while I went to the hospital with Kirk. Several hours later, Gavin came out of surgery and we loaded him on the team bus, asleep. The sun was up by the time we rolled into Toronto. The Marlboros had won the game, and the Ottawa defenseman who clipped Gavin never did set his skates back on the ice that night.

The 1970-71 edition of the Toronto Marlboros was very good, and the future looked exceptional. Gardner, Harris and Shutt were just flying, combining for 342 points through the regular season. All the boys were playing their hearts out. The regular season had seen the Marlies finish in fifth spot, but we defeated the first place Peterborough Petes in the playoffs to earn a shot at the Memorial Cup. We were in Montreal for a game against the Junior Canadiens, the previous year's Memorial Cup champions. The excitement level was comparable to an NHL match between Montreal and Toronto. The series was sensational, and we went into the seventh game tied, three games apiece. In the deciding game, the third period was winding down and we were down a goal when the Montreal fans began harassing our bench, screaming and throwing cups and small items, including batteries at us. Our team was livid, as was the Montreal Forum staff. Then, the police ordered both teams off the ice. We weren't sure exactly what was going on, but we were horrified to discover that a fan, just a few rows behind our bench had been found with a gun. The police removed a number of fans and settled the crowd down, but our team was never able to regain its composure, and we lost our chance for the Memorial Cup by that single goal.

The next morning, I walked into Stafford's office and was greeted with, "Get lost. You threw it away." I bolted out the door and went to see Jim Gregory's. I explained my disappointment with the Marlboros loss and how Stafford had screamed at me and thrown me out of his office. Jim put a fatherly arm around my shoulder and explained. "Just calm down, Tom. Your dad is just as upset as you are, but he doesn't know the right way to say it." Jim left and returned within minutes with Harold Ballard in tow. Ballard had many nice things to say about all that the team had accomplished that year, and how upsetting it was for everyone that the Marlboros had been so close, but so far away at the same time. It was the last time Harold would speak to me in kind tones, and that remains a pleasant memory. He asked me to hang on, and reappeared with my dad, whom he insisted apologize. I accepted, but was admittedly discouraged and a piece of my heart was taken away that day, never to return.

The final season Stafford presided over the Leafs was 1970-71. In 1969-70, the team had struggled dismally, finishing dead last in the East Division Before the new season began, the Leafs decided they needed to shore up their goaltending, and they acquired Jacques Plante, who had spent the previous year with the St. Louis Blues. Through the years, I'd watched Plante stone the Leafs time after time, and never liked him. Oh sure, I loved the way he played — he was very fast and as entertaining as any goalie in the league, but he was very hard on the Leafs. I insisted that I be at his first Leafs practice. I arrived at the Gardens early, and I wasn't alone. More sports reporters and curious on-lookers than I'd seen in years at a practise accompanied me. After a very sound workout, Jacques pulled aside the team's four main defensemen and spoke to them briefly. Then, he went to the Leafs trainer, Joe Sgro, and asked him to bring 100 pucks to the blueline. Each defensemen positioned himself in a row across the blueline, and cradled 25 pucks. Jim McKenny was by the boards facing Jacques to the left. Mike Pelyk was next to him on the blueline, but closer to the centre of the ice. Rick Ley was on the blueline on the other side of centre, while Jim Dorey was on the boards facing Plante to the right. Jacques asked them to rapidly fire the pucks at him, alternating from side to side, starting with McKenny, then Dorey, back to the left to Pelyk, then Ley to the right, and repeated until all 100 pucks had been fired. Each shot was to follow its predecessor by about a second, so that all the pucks would be shot in just under two minutes.

All of the onlookers in the arena were as incredulous as me. Jacques would quickly position himself just outside the crease on the side from where the shot would come. As soon as the stick hit the puck, Plante knew whether it would be on net or not. If it was going wide, he didn't wait until the puck hit the end boards, but immediately shifted to prepare himself for the next shot. He'd ignore some of the pucks fired at him, and they'd ding off the crossbar or hit the goal post. If they were on net, he deftly used his blocker or pads to angle the puck off into the corner, or use his stick to steer the puck away. But he never let a single shot in. From time to time, he'd make a curious move: he'd catch a puck, toss it up to his side, then knock it up over the glass with his stick. I counted the pucks Plante knocked over the glass and, curious, retrieved them from the seats afterwards. There were 16 pucks; each chipped.

When the "Hundred-Second Exercise" was completed, spontaneous cheers erupted throughout the stands and among the players who had gathered by the bench to watch. McKenny, Dorey, Pelyk and Ley rushed over to Jacques, hooting and slapping their sticks on the ice in appreciation of what they'd just witnessed. I lined the 16 chipped pucks along the bench. Jacques skated over to me, lifting his mask and smiling broadly. In his charming accent, he glanced at the pucks, then at me and asked, "So, Tommy — have you learned anything?" I said, "I'm sure I did. But I'm not sure what it was." Jacques laughed, "Tom, you and me are going to share a secret, okay? And this stays a secret until after I retire." Curiously, I agreed.

Jacques began. "I'm a lucky man, Tommy. My skill comes mostly from my eyes." He admitted that physical talents were important too, but it was his vision that made him great. "I can see where the stick hits the puck — toe, heel or centre of the stick, and I have learned to react to that and know where the puck is going to go," he said. "I can tell from the second a puck is hit whether it's coming at me or going wide, and I've got it now so that I know if a puck is even going to hit a post or a crossbar."

"Those chipped pucks you picked up wobble in the air erratically and are the real reason I invented the facemask." I then followed Jacques to the Leafs dressing room and listened to him further is goaltending lesson. He explained how he broke-in his equipment and traveled with his gloves, never letting them out of sight. He spoke of how he mentally prepared himself for games and focused while on the ice. Many around the Leafs found Jacques Plante a little bit withdrawn from the team. But he and I became great friends, and I anxiously listened any time Jacques wanted to offer a lesson. With Jacques in net, the Leafs were back in the playoffs in 1970-71. The next year, he shared duties with, Bernie Parent and the team made the playoffs once again. Plante's final year in Toronto was 1972-73, and he finished his NHL career with the Boston Bruins. Like many, I was upset when he was traded — I thought he deserved the right to retire in the blue and white of the Toronto Maple Leafs.

Chapter Sixteen

Tax Evasion

The Hot Stove Lounge was where I ate most of my meals. Many were with my new wife Anne, the young lady I had started to date after the Marlboros team party celebrating our 1966-67 Memorial Cup victory. We were married a few years later in 1969, the year I turned 23. Other times I ate with my hockey friends Jim Gregory, King Clancy or Harold Ballard. Meals with Jim Gregory were often working meals, and although they became less frequent as Jim's responsibilities grew, they were always important to me. Dinners with King were also very special, and certainly a lot of fun. No one was as loyal to the blue and white of the Leafs as King Clancy. When he died at the age of 83 in 1986, they should have buried his heart at centre ice of Maple Leaf Gardens.

With Harold, the conversations during meals usually gave me insight into all the concerts that were being planned for the Gardens. The list was so impressive; a virtual who's who of music history — the Beatles, the Monkees, Frank Sinatra, Rod Stewart, the Beach Boys, the Rolling Stones, the Guess Who, James Brown, the Tijuana Brass, Jimi Hendrix, Johnny Cash, Tom Jones, Blood, Sweat and Tears and Led Zeppelin, to name but a few. This was wildly exciting for a young man like me, and Harold made certain that his kids and I met almost all of them. His son, Bill Ballard, began his professional career going to these concerts at Maple Leaf Gardens, and eventually booked them himself. Bill, along with his partners Michael Cohl and David Wolinsky, owned and ran Concert Productions International as a Maple Leaf gardens subsidiary beginning in the summer of 1973. They bought the company outright the next year. For 20 years, CPI was Canada's largest concert promotion firm. To this day, Bill is still responsible for the Rolling Stones world tours with his new company, T.N.A. (The Next Adventure). Bill also manages Canadian singer John McDermott.

I especially enjoyed the opportunity to share a meal with my dad at the Hot Stove and talk hockey, or when time permitted, reminisce of my childhood years. Curiously I began to note my father would order a drink with his lunch. My Dad had never drank until the age of 35. My grandfather never touched alcohol, and I guess that Dad picked up his abstinence from him. But another reason Dad limited his drinking was because of his asthma. Stafford was constantly spraying his throat in an effort to suppress the coughing and ease the irritation. Little did he realize that the medicinal spray eased the discomfort, but also caused irreparable damage to his esophagus.

My father was struggling with many troubling issues towards the end of his life. He was intent on rebuilding the Toronto Maple Leafs, but cash flow was a sizeable concern. My father was losing money on a jet he used for the Gardens business. He was buried in a mountain of invoices that went back to the mid-'60s, and there were whispers within the building of improprieties with the invoices. Dad was seeing bills and cash fly everywhere for work done to the Gardens, to his new house and to Harold Ballard's house. There was also a farm near Guelph that Dad and Mom were restoring, and that was taking an inordinate amount of time and money. My father was having trouble sleeping and his health began to deteriorate.

Harold tried to settle Stafford down with an arm around his shoulder and a perennial, "Don't worry, Staff." But Dad was worried and, after a few years, Harold dragged Dad down to the Hot Stove for a few drinks. As the years and troubles grew, so did the alcohol consumption. The social drinking intensified, and the occasional drink became a nightly occurrence. After a while, Dad would drink during the day too. My Mom was very concerned, and I attempted to intervene. A new part of my job description around Maple Leaf Gardens became chauffeur to the president. I would wait around the Hot Stove after work, trying to get Dad out of the club and home safely. I'm sure that watching this night after night helped reinforce my decision to abstain from drinking.

Harold never really seemed to be too concerned about Dad's drinking. As time went on, Ballard asked, "Hey Staff, do you have a will? I just had one done, and I can help walk you through it." Dad mumbled that no, he didn't have one, and he'd appreciate Harold's help in having one made up. Unfortunately, I was not at the table at the time. If I had been, my life and Maple Leaf Gardens history would have been very different.

Harold Ballard, who dictated the details to his lawyer, John Edison, wrote the last will and testament of C. Stafford Smythe. The specific details made certain that my Mom and the four children would be taken care of. But the point of contention was that Harold made himself executor to the will, and threw in a paragraph that would allow him to buy Dad's shares upon Stafford's death.

Ballard slipped the will to Stafford late one night after Dad had had far too much to drink. With a cursory glance, my father signed it on January 4, 1971. The witnesses were staff from the Hot Stove Lounge. And oddly, the will was not legally registered until after my father's death. The signed legal will was put away and never discussed with anyone in the Smythe family. Dad never gave the document another thought until it was too late. This single incident was the most serious error of Smythe family history.

As the Gardens made more profit, Dad and Harold Ballard got involved in some activities they clearly shouldn't have. For one, they set up a fictitious bank account under the name S.H. Marlie, and money from the Canadian Amateur Hockey Association and the Ontario Hockey Association, money, which was intended for the Toronto Marlboros, was deposited into it. The signing officers of the account were my father and Harold, and money was withdrawn for the personal use of Harold and Stafford. The "S" stood for "Stafford," "H" for "Harold" and the "Marlie" was actually the common nickname of the Marlboros. The two also had a penthouse apartment in the Village Green Apartments, just a block away from the Gardens. The unit was a convenient oasis from the pressures of Maple Leaf Gardens, and afforded Stafford, Harold and other members of the Silver Seven the opportunity to enjoy a respite from their normal routine. The penthouse apartment was registered to the Marlboro Athletic Club.

In August 1965, Cloke Construction began to do renovations on Maple Leaf Gardens, reconfiguring the arena to include more seats. But in October of that same year, Cloke also began to do renovations to the Ballard house on Montgomery Road in Etobicoke, and to build Mom and Dad a new home on Ashley Park not far away. All the invoices for work done by Cloke Construction at all three locations were sent to Maple Leaf Gardens and signed by the Gardens' accounting staff. Some of the invoices clearly defined work done at the homes of both my father and Ballard. Yet, they were signed off with explanations, which identified work done at the Gardens.

Dad sifted through the invoices, sometimes finding double and triple invoices for the same thing. The matter was so complex, and my father got more upset by the minute. Finally, Stafford realized he needed to find an accountant who could straighten out the tangled financial mess. Dad hired Donald Crump, who still sits on the Leafs advisory board to this day.

From day one, Crump dug in, working exhaustive hours in an effort to make heads or tails out of the invoices. Finally, he threw up his hands and called Harold and Stafford in for an extended and very candid conversation. There were problems-big problems — and Crump explained that they could quite possibly be charged with income tax evasion. Don felt that through his connections, he could let the Department of National Revenue know what had been going on and explain that both principals were aware of errors that had been made. Dad and Harold could then ask for National Revenue's help in properly lining up all the financial details, and offer to pay any extra taxation required. Stafford and Harold agreed to the plan and kept their fingers crossed.

Two days later, all hell broke loose. It was October 1968 when the Royal Canadian Mounted Police and the Department of National Revenue burst into Maple Leaf Gardens, the Ballard home and my Mom and Dad's house. They seized everything relevant they could find. Everywhere I turned in the Gardens that day, the staff was in tears. I hurried home to see my Mom, and she was hysterical. National Revenue agents and RCMP officers were all through her house, pulling things apart, looking for damning evidence against my father. During it all, my mother's biggest fear was the negative effects this incident would have against my father's already questionable health.

Donald Crump's connections at the Department of National Revenue certainly hadn't helped get co-operation. Although both families were visibly upset, Ballard's concerned diminished soon thereafter and he found humour in the entire incident. The Smythes however, have a difficultly discussing the dark time, even today.

Dad searched for the best legal-counsel available, and hired J.J. Robinette, a distinguished Canadian defense lawyer. Robinette went through all the books, simultaneously interviewing virtually everyone at Maple Leaf Gardens and at Cloke Construction. After numerous weeks of constant study, Robinette called a hasty meeting with Ballard and my Dad, and let them know that he felt there was absolutely no chance for winning this case.

As much as the senior executives attempted to keep the pending problems away from the day-to-day operation of the Gardens, the rumours spread like wildfire. The third member of the Toronto Maple Leafs ownership group, John Bassett, distanced himself from Stafford and Harold. He had committed no improprieties, and feared that guilt by association could damage his personal reputation as well as that of the Toronto Telegram and CFTO-TV. Any unlawful conduct could jeopardize his broadcasting license.

John Bassett called an emergency board meeting on June 26, 1969 to discuss removing my father and Ballard from their respective managing director and presidential positions. It was held at Imperial Oil's boardroom, a neutral location outside the Gardens. Only 15 of the 20 directors attended. Many of them argued that Stafford and Harold should step down from their positions until the legalities had been finalized, but my father's lawyer advised him and Harold that by doing so, they would be perceived as admitting their guilt. The arguments got very heated and accusatory, and finally, John Bassett called for a secret ballot to decide on the executive fate of Stafford and Harold.

In parliamentary procedure, the chairman does not have a vote, unless the tally results in a tie. Sure enough, of the 14 voting members on the board, seven voted in favour of retaining Dad and Harold. Seven voted for their dismissal. As chairman, John Bassett had to cast the deciding vote. Bassett chose to remove Dad and Harold from their positions at Maple Leaf Gardens. Silver Seven member George Mara was installed as the new president.

Harold and my father intended to reinstate themselves as president and vice-president of Maple Leaf Gardens by ridding themselves of many of the board members, specifically those who had voted against them. They called in favours from some of the shareholders who carried a fair bit of weight. Most of those who attended the annual shareholders meeting in December 1970 voted with Harold and Stafford. Of the 20 members on the Maple Leafs board, 16 were removed. The only four remaining board members were Paul McNamara, who stayed on the Leafs board until 1990, my father's good friend Terry Jeffries and two others — Harold Ballard and Stafford Smythe. John Bassett resigned. So did George Mara. All of the other members of the Silver Seven were gone.

Previous to his resignation, John Bassett tried to wrestle control of the Gardens away from Ballard and my father. By currying favours with shareholders and trying to buy more shares for himself, Bassett gave gaining control a valiant effort. But the Toronto Telegram was struggling badly. There was considerable union trouble, and whispers in the newsrooms said that the paper was on its last legs. Where there's smoke, you'll often find fire, and the Toronto Telegram folded shortly thereafter. From its ashes sprang a phoenix called the Toronto Sun. Bassett relinquished his fight for control, leaving Stafford and Ballard as co-owners of the Toronto Maple Leafs. Dad and Harold spent $5.5 million of borrowed money to buy out John Bassett's shares in Maple Leaf Gardens. In 10 years of ownership, John Bassett Jr. made approximately $7 million on an investment of $900,000.

On July 9, 1969, Stafford and Harold were charged with income tax evasion. The charges alleged that between April 1965 and March 1968, my father not only appropriated $208,166 from Maple Leaf Gardens for construction on his new house, a cottage and on his farm, but also did not declare the income. All told, they alleged that my father had taken $35,178 from Maple Leaf Gardens for personal and family expenses. In addition,

$35,575 was the stated amount taken from the Toronto Marlboros for personal and family expenses. Four other counts alleged that my father submitted false or deceptive income tax returns for 1964, 1965, 1966 and 1967.

Allegations towards Harold Ballard were similar. He was charged with misappropriating $74,395 from Maple Leaf Gardens for renovations on his home and on his cottage on Georgian Bay, all undeclared as income. And Ballard apparently took $24,713 for personal and family expenses from the Gardens. Allegedly, he made off with $35,575 from the Toronto Marlboros for personal and family expenses. Harold Ballard was charged with submitting false or deceptive income tax returns for the same years as my father.

If Dad and Harold were convicted, they'd be facing a prison term of anywhere between two months and five years and fines as high as $10,000. In addition, a penalty could be added which would be up to double the amount of taxes evaded.

J.J. Robinette made his point clearly: he would not take on the case unless Harold and Stafford agreed to make a deal, which would involve one to two years in jail. Harold felt they should face the sentence and get it over with, then proceed with their lives, but Dad was very upset, worrying about the shame a jail sentence would bring to the Smythe name, and the shadow that would fall across the Toronto Maple Leafs. And there was further bad news. Mr. Robinette informed Dad that the throat spray for his asthma was from the United States and would not be allowed in a Canadian prison.

Stafford deliberated, and finally told Robinette to proceed with the deal. But in one of the quiet moments Dad and I shared at that time, my father let me know that he would die before going to jail. How prophetic that statement would become.

Anne and I lived for a time in Rosedale, one of Toronto's most desirable neighbourhoods, with its heritage homes and streets shrouded in the branches of 100-year-old oak trees. Our home was at Sherbourne North and Maple Avenue, not far from Yonge and Bloor. In the fall of 1970, Stafford, Dot, Anne and I were invited to a cocktail party near our home that included John Turner on its guest list. At the time, Turner was minister of justice in Pierre Trudeau's Liberal government and was involved in Stafford and Harold's income tax evasion charges. The Smythes were long-time supporters of the Progressive Conservative party. Stafford waited until there was an opportunity to get Turner alone and whispered, "Look John, if I support you and you are elected, would you be willing to strike a deal so I won't have to go to jail?" Turner glanced around to make certain no one was within earshot, and said, "Sorry Staff, but I'm using your tax evasion case as a stepping stone to move myself up in the government." Turner did not see me standing quietly behind them, unnoticed, hanging on every word that John Turner said to my father.

Turner displayed a great deal of interest in prosecuting my Dad, much greater than what he applied toward Ballard. Stafford, an avowed Progressive Conservative, had often fought with the Liberal party and it was rumoured that Turner considered my father's attitude towards the tax evasion charges too cavalier.

After years of battling breast cancer, Harold Ballard's wife Dorothy died on December 2, 1969. What had been a dreadful year already for the Ballard and Smythe families just got worse. Harold and his children, as well as Stafford, Dorothea, my sister Vicky and I, had all tried hard to keep Dorothy Ballard comfortable during her final months, and offered help to Harold in any way possible. The Smythes and the Ballards had been very close up to that point. Mom and Dad regularly socialized with Harold and Dorothy, Mary Liz and Vicky were great friends and Bill, Bobby and I were close.

The saddest thing about losing Dorothy Ballard was that things were never the same between our families. Our lives moved along and changed. Harold slowly withdrew. He still worked hard around the Gardens, probably even harder than he had in the past, but he changed, and if you weren't there every day, the change was so gradual that you might not notice it.

It saddened me that Harold and I we're no longer close. Whenever I would ask his opinion on hockey decisions, he'd simply reply, "Go ahead," and that would be the extent of the conversation. When we were kids, my father and Harold always joked with the Ballard kids and me. Harold would say, in his former life, he was a pirate, and we'd laugh about it, but now, I shuddered to think that Harold was truly beginning to feel that way.

Chapter Seventeen

Persecuted to Death by His Enemies

The Maple Leafs owned a Lear Jet, registered to both Stafford Smythe and Harold Ballard, which, was used for scouting expeditions and various other purposes. When the jet was used for business matters, invoices were billed to Maple Leaf Gardens. Stafford and Harold paid for their own personal flights such as; those, Dad took to his Muskoka cottage or Florida home, from time to time.

Once, there was a need for a quick trip to Buffalo to evaluate a player the Leafs were looking to acquire. Chief Scout Bob Davidson, general manager Punch Imlach as well as King Clancy and Stafford climbed into the plane, and the pilot took off across Lake Ontario. Within minutes, King glanced out the window and started screaming, "Fire! Fire!" Clancy was crossing himself, begging salvation, when the pilot yelled back, "I'm aware of the situation, and we're making every attempt to put out the fire." The pilot made a quick U-turn that had the Leaf passengers clutching on to their seats. The pilot had shut down the flaming engine, and was racing back to Toronto Airport. They landed safely, but not without fire engines spraying the plane as they braked down the runway. Dad had to help King off the plane, and after he descended the steps, crossing himself all the while, Clancy knelt and kissed the ground.

The plane was isolated with yellow police tape, and within two weeks, an investigation revealed that the plane had been sabotaged. Something had been poured into the fuel that ignited the flames. All the passengers were terrified. My Dad visibly distraught grew very distant and quiet. King, who had been the most frightened passenger on the flight, tried to lighten up the mood at Maple Leaf Gardens with jokes and banter about the plane. He loved to tease Harold, "Hey, how come you weren't on that plane?"

During the summer of 1971, my mother and father used the jet to make the nine-minute flight to their cottage in Muskoka. Regular road travel would be the equivalent of two or more hours. On one such journey, my parents' jet landed, and Mom and Dad drove along HWY 118 from the airfield to the cottage. While passing through the small northern town of Bracebridge, someone threw a glass bottle at their car, shattering the windshield. Mom was a mess, and Dad was visibly shaken. Not being able to see through the windshield, Dad drove very slowly, his head hanging out of the driver's side window. Maneuvering through the town's streets, my mother and father found a gas station and went in to see if they could replace the windshield. The mechanic didn't have a spare, but he took out part of the windshield on the driver's side, and taped up the rest so it wouldn't collapse. The mechanic was aghast, and apologized profusely on behalf of the citizens of Bracebridge. My father felt that someone was out to get him.

Clayton Powell was the special prosecutor for the Ontario Attorney General's office. Through 1969 and into 1971, Powell's team interviewed almost 200 people concerning the business practices of Stafford and Harold Ballard. Many believed that some of the Leaf players who were friends with Powell, let him know what was happening from the inside. In July 1971, while working in his office, my father was arrested on charges of defrauding Maple Leaf Gardens of $249,000. He was taken to Metro Toronto Police headquarters on Jarvis Street, where he was fingerprinted and photographed for a mug shot. Dad's lawyer suggested he be released on his own recognizance, but Provincial Judge P.J. Bolsby put the bail at $50,000. King Clancy was with me when my father was released. Ballard was at his cottage when he found out that the police were looking to arrest him as well. He phoned them, and said he'd meet them at his Etobicoke house. Police charged Ballard with defrauding the Gardens of $82,000. And the partners were charged jointly with the theft of $146,000 in cash and securities, mostly from cheques deposited in the S.H. Marlie account between 1964 and 1969.

Dad fell into a tailspin from which he'd never emerge. The drinking accelerated and Dad's health declined. By September, the Gardens was buzzing with preparations for the upcoming hockey season. Dad was as focused on the season as I had ever seen him, in spite of his poor health and the looming court case with the Department of National Revenue. On the weekend before the season's opening night, I drove him home from the Gardens. Dad seemed very ill — his asthma spray was reacting badly with the alcohol, and he was coughing heavily and vomiting. He mentioned to me that he should probably get a new, updated will. No mention was made of the will prepared by Harold Ballard and his lawyer. When I suggested that my first girlfriend's father, Jim Karfilis, could help him out with it, Dad said, "Yes, let's get it done right away." Karfilis worked very quickly to get the will completed, but Dad's illness and his agitated mental state made completion take longer than expected.

Grandpa spent a fair bit of time with my Dad. They talked Smythe talk — the Maple Leafs, and of his kids and grandchildren. Dad said something to Conn, which he had also said to me. "See Dad? I told you they wouldn't put me in jail." That statement haunts each one of the family members when we think of Dad.

On the morning of October 12, 1971, I arrived for work at Maple Leaf Gardens and as the normal went to say good morning to my Dad. I searched everywhere, but couldn't find him. I asked Ballard if he'd seen him around, and he told me, "Hold on, I might know where he is." He called me 20 minutes later. "Tom, your father's being loaded into an ambulance headed for Wellesley Hospital. I found him on the floor, and there was blood everywhere." Rushing over to Wellesley, I was told that my Dad was in emergency surgery with a bleeding ulcer, and that I was instructed to wait in the waiting room. From there, I phoned my Mom, my sisters and some of the folks from the Gardens. We spent a long, anxious afternoon together, waiting for word on Dad's fate.

At last, the surgeon came into the waiting area, and addressed the family. "Mrs. Smythe," he cautiously proceeded, "Your husband has survived the surgery, but he's in very critical condition. We have repaired the ulcers in his stomach, but there has been substantial blood loss. Mr. Smythe is critically low on blood and we need to build it back up to where it belongs. Unfortunately, his blood type, O Negative, is quite rare. We could use some volunteers to donate blood for us." Virtually everyone in the waiting area found a pay phone, and armed with a handful of dimes, began calling everyone we knew.

Mom waited to see Dad with my older sister Vicky and me. The rest left for home, leaving us with thoughts and prayers for my father. Close to 11 o'clock that evening, Mom and I were taken in to see Dad. We were horrified to see the once strong Stafford connected to numerous tubes, IVs, monitors and machines to aid his breathing and heart rate. My uncle, Dad's younger brother, Dr. Hugh Smythe, kindly suggested we go home. "Stafford has a long way to go. Go get some sleep and I'll call you both if anything changes."

It didn't take long. My phone rang at 4:00 in the morning. It was Hugh. "Tommy, your Dad is coughing up blood again and has been rushed back into surgery. They've had to remove a substantial portion of his stomach. I've already called your mother and she's on her way." I don't know how I did it, but I got to Wellesley Hospital by 4:15. Mom was just arriving too. Uncle Hugh told us that as the blood pressure built back up to where it belonged, blood began to pour from Dad's esophagus and a vein in his stomach, and things looked bleak. I was taken into the critical recovery room at 4:30, my eyes damp with tears. There laid Dad, tubes in his mouth and over his nose. I knew he couldn't talk, but I watched his eyes dart from machine to machine, and I clutched his hand. "Dad? Don't be frightened. Hold my hand and look at me. Squeeze my hand and promise me that you won't give up." My father squeezed my hand, and with each minute that passed, he squeezed a little harder. Mom and I sat there quietly, both unable to speak, then, suddenly, Dad's hand went limp. The alarm went off, and my father's heart monitor registered a straight line.

On October 13, 1971, Maple Leaf Gardens issued a statement: "With great sorrow we announce the passing of our president, C. Stafford Smythe, who died this morning. The body will be resting at his home, 15 Ashley Park Road, in Etobicoke. Funeral services will be held in St. Paul's Anglican Church, Bloor and Jarvis Streets, at 1pm, Thursday, October 14. In lieu of flowers, kindly send donations to the charity of your choice."

The funeral was extremely emotional. I served as a pallbearer along with my Uncle Hugh, the Maple Leafs general manager and our dear friend Jim Gregory, Dad's long-time partner Harold Ballard, George Mara, and Terry Jeffries, Dad's great friend from the Gardens' board of directors. George Armstrong and Bob Baun, representing the Toronto Maple Leafs' players, were also pallbearers.

Dad was buried in his beloved Muskoka, a calming place where he truly found the peace he craved. His gravesite is in the yard of Christ Anglican Church, overlooking the Joseph River where he can watch the boats pass forever.

My mother and I selected a large rock, and had it split to be a Muskoka tombstone. Mom very kindly let me write the epitaph:

"Here lies Conn Stafford Smythe, Lieut. RCNVR 1940-1944. He was dearly beloved of his wife, children and many friends. He was persecuted to death by his enemies. Now he sleeps in the quiet north country that loved him for the person he truly was. Born Toronto March 15, 1921. Died October 13, 1971."

I chose to ride in the hearse, to be with my father, my friend on his last ride to Muskoka. I was devastated. I didn't know how I would bear life without him. My long-time friend, the late Rick Porter drove. As the car turned onto Highway 401, Rick said, "Tommy, you haven't eaten for what, two whole days?" He leaned over and popped open the glove compartment. It was jammed full of snacks. Rick pulled out a cooler filled with ice-cold Coke. It was a small thing to him, but I appreciated it as one of the many thoughtful things the Porter family from one of Toronto's most recognized funeral homes, Turner and Porter Funeral Directors, has done for the Smythe family.

NHL games have been postponed only a handful of times. Chicago and Montreal cancelled their games on January 28, 1936 when King George VI died. President John F. Kennedy's assassination caused the cancellation of a Detroit-Boston game on November 24, 1963. Three games were postponed on April 7, 1968, when civil rights leader Martin Luther King was gunned down. And Harold Ballard postponed the game scheduled against the Detroit Red Wings on October 13, 1971 due to my father's death. This was the first and only time in Maple Leaf history that a game had been postponed. It was scheduled instead for November 1.

Chapter Eighteen

End of an Era

My Dad died 12 days before he was scheduled to go on trial. On his death, Harold Ballard was appointed president of the Toronto Maple Leafs. He repaid Maple Leaf Gardens the money he had taken, and paid the income tax as demanded by the government. As a result, the tax evasion charges were dropped, but Clayton Powell proceeded with the theft and fraud charges. When Ballard finally stood trial in May 1972, J.J. Robinette was proven right — Harold Ballard and my father hadn't stood a chance. Powell held all the cards. His witnesses paraded in front of the judge with one damning piece of evidence after another.

On August 15, County Court Judge Harry Deyman convicted Harold Ballard on 47 of the 49 charges of fraud and theft of money, goods and services in the amount of $205,000. Sentencing was scheduled for September 7, 1972. Alan Eagleson phoned the Judge to ask if the sentencing could be postponed until later in the year so that Harold could attend the 1972 Summit Series between Canada and the USSR. Judge Deyman agreed, but was angered by the intervention from Ballard's friends. As a result, Harold received a more severe sentence than expected when he returned to court on October 20. The 69-year old Ballard was sentenced to two concurrent three-year sentences, one for theft and the other for fraud. He was taken to Millhaven Correctional Institute, a minimum-security prison near Kingston, two hours east of Toronto.

After only serving one year of his sentence, Harold was released on parole and returned to Maple Leaf Gardens. He had continued to run the Gardens from jail, using his son Bill as the conduit. Ballard's prison term was anything but difficult. It's rumoured that his cell was more like a luxurious hotel suite and that Ballard played golf most days, ate terrific meals and entertained prison staff in his cell. He was often granted day passes and at one point left Kingston and returned to Toronto for six days during the Leafs signing of Darryl Sittler.

Harold Ballard had never before run a hockey team. Through his many years tied to teams like the Sea Fleas, the Marlboros and the Leafs, Harold took care of finances and some public relations, in addition to helping the executives in whatever way he could. My grandfather and dad had been the ones who oversaw the hockey operation of any team with which they'd been involved. They scouted, coached and cajoled from the bench, and motivated from the dressing room. Running the Toronto Maple Leafs was going to be a new experience for Harold, and I was anxious to see how he would do.

Following my father's death, I was called in to listen to the reading of his will. The reading took place in the boardroom of Ballard's lawyer, John Edison. I was the only one from my family to attend. My godfather, Terry Jeffries, a pallbearer at my Dad's funeral and Stafford's life-long friend, was also in attendance. Terry was Dad's partner in a holding company that owned half of Maple Leaf Gardens' controlling shares. Jeffries had also been a board member of the Gardens from 1963 to 1970. Edison and Ballard said hello to Jeffries, then Edison condescendingly said, "Hello Tom. I guess you are here to find out how rich you are going to be." I was outraged. "That is the last thing I'm interested in. I'm here to protect the Smythe family," I snapped.

Terry Jeffries and I listened to the reading of the will with stiff upper lips. At the end, Terry stood up and ranted, "That will is outrageous. I am still Stafford's partner, and will not have my name connected to this mess." He strutted out of the boardroom, and never again spoke to Harold Ballard. Terry Jeffries decided he had had enough, and moved right out of the city. He lives a reclusive lifestyle on a 100-acre, heavily wooded property up in the Muskokas. Another great friend of my father's took a similar route. Around this time, Jack Stafford sold Stafford Industries, his chocolate syrup and confections business, and moved to Mont Tremblant, Quebec. He too had had enough of Toronto after Stafford's death.

Harold Ballard and John Edison requested a $100,000 advance payment each as executors of the will. After this was announced, one of the judges, a former amateur hockey player from Toronto named Joseph Kane, called me into a quiet side room reserved for judges. "Tom," he started, "all the judges are furious about this will, and we're all fighting amongst ourselves to see who is going to be the one lucky enough to oversee this case. You, your mother and her lawyer should just sit quietly at the back of the courtroom. We'll look after this." The judge reprimanded Ballard and Edison for the ridiculous executors' request. A hundred thousand dollars in 1971 is equivalent to a million dollars today. Both were chastised for their greed, and then ordered out of court. Mom, her lawyer Ralf McCreath, and I chuckled quietly as we zipped out the back door and saw the press surrounding Harold and Edison.

My father's assets included the house on Ashley Park, the summer cottage in Muskoka and the farm he'd been working on near Guelph, as well as cash, stocks and bonds. Dad's will ensured that Mom would be extremely comfortable for the rest of her life. After my Dad's death, Mom sold the home on Ashley Park. At the age of 50, Dot went back to school in New York, where she took interior design courses. With my mother doing the designing and my sister Vicky taking care of the books, the two started their own business: Dorothea Smythe Design.

My father was very generous to my three sisters and me. None of us were very old: Vicky and I were in our mid-20s, Mary had just turned 20 and Elizabeth was only 16. The three girls would receive their money as soon as my Dad's assets were liquefied. But the will stated that my money was to be held for a 10-year period. It wasn't that I wanted or needed my father's money, but I wanted to remain a partner in the ownership of Maple Leaf Gardens as I had always been promised. By holding back my money, I was no threat to challenge Ballard for ownership. Uncle Hugh and I tried to mount a campaign to purchase the Gardens, but found raising the money difficult. I had some money of my own, but the money from my father's estate was out of reach, and the banks gave me a difficult time in my pursuit to borrow against something I couldn't touch for 10 years. Each day, Harold would send someone down to ask how the move to purchase was going. I bluffed, and always said, "Things are looking better each day." In turn, he got nervous, and we drove the price up from $5.5 million to the final $7 million price Ballard ultimately paid the Smythes for my father's shares.

Dad's will stated that if one of the partners died, or wanted to sell his shares and be removed from Maple Leaf Gardens ownership, his shares must first be offered to the other partner. As executor of Stafford's will, Harold Ballard took advantage of this opportunity. He simply bought Stafford's 251,545 shares in Maple Leaf Gardens with a $7-million bank loan. My Uncle Hugh, in resignation, offered to sell his 1,200 Gardens shares to Harold. Ballard eagerly bought the lot. Harold then insisted that my uncle turn in his season's tickets. Uncle Hugh did, and has only returned to Maple Leaf Gardens twice — once to pick up my grandfather's belongings after Conn died in November 1980, and then to watch the final game at Maple Leaf Gardens, February 13th, 1999. As the former team doctor, Hugh would have treated most of the Leaf alumni present at that final game.

Ballard's holding company, Harold E. Ballard Ltd., now owned more than 70 percent of the Gardens. Unfortunately, I learned that Harold Ballard was the new owner of Maple Leaf Gardens while driving, listening to my car radio. It was a devastating way to find out that the Smythes would no longer be behind the Toronto Maple Leafs and Maple Leaf Gardens. From my grandfather's initial purchase of the Toronto St. Patricks in 1927, his vision and construction of Maple Leaf Gardens in 1931, the uncertain war years, the turnover of ownership to my father and for each of the franchise's 11 Stanley Cups, the Smythes had run the Toronto Maple Leafs. But as of February 4, 1972, the Smythe name was tragically no longer tied to the Toronto Maple Leafs and Maple Leaf Gardens.

Chapter Nineteen

Poor Sports and Sporting Goods

When Maple Leaf Gardens was erected, the building contained not only a world-class arena, but several other shops and services as well. Facing Carlton Street on the west side was Olympia Recreation. There, fans could enjoy a game of bowling or shoot a round of billiards. The Leafs captain during the 1930's owned the Happy Day Pharmacy, in the Gardens at 50 Carlton. The main entrance to the Gardens was at 60 Carlton Street. At 62 Carlton was Love & Bennett Sporting Goods. On the corner of Carlton and Church was the United Cigar Store. And along Church Street inside the Gardens were J.J. Connors Beauty Parlour Supplies and the Junior League Opportunity Shop.

Although the name and ownership changed through the years, it's at Love & Bennett Sporting Goods that I spent the early 1970s. The store remained at 62 Carlton Street until 1947, at which time McCutcheon's Cameras moved in to that prime location. Meanwhile in 1944, Doug Laurie, a well-known Toronto sports supporter, opened a sporting goods store around the corner. Doug Laurie Sports stayed in that location until 1963, at which point it moved over to the newly vacant 62 Carlton location. The Hot Stove Lounge, private members' restaurant, was created in the location that Doug Laurie vacated.

During the late 1960s, Doug Laurie and I would often talk about his impending retirement. When he mentioned that the time was growing closer, I privately asked him if he would consider selling me the 60 shares he owned in Maple Leaf Gardens; shares he had owned since the Gardens opened. He agreed that when the day of his retirement came, he would sell his shares — now worth a small fortune — to me at market value. Laurie's 60 original shares had split numerous times since the 30s and were actually worth the equivalent of thousands of shares.

In January 1971, the late Harry Addison Jr., Bill Ballard and I talked about a combined ownership of Doug Laurie Sporting Goods. Our agreement included a buy-sell arrangement whereby one partner could purchase the business outright from the other partners, at fair market value. Harold's oldest son, Bill Ballard, was a lawyer and he drew up the complete offer for Laurie. The three of us met with Laurie and discussed his retirement and sale of his business. "It looks good boys, but let me sleep on it overnight, and we'll talk again tomorrow," concluded Laurie. I quickly added, "Mr. Laurie, don't forget about our agreement for me to purchase your Gardens shares." Bill Ballard leapt to his feet, pounded his fist on the table and screamed, "Why don't I know about this? Why can't I buy those shares for myself?" Laurie made his exit. "Let's just sleep on it tonight, and we'll discuss things further tomorrow," he said. The second Doug closed the door Bill continued his rant. "Forget it! I don't want to have any part in this business with you," he said, and stormed out of the room.

He didn't speak to either Harry or I for a long time. I didn't really comprehend why Bill was so angry about the shares until after my dad died. Then, the reason glared at me: the Ballards were attempting to take over controlling shares of Maple Leaf Gardens. The plot was right there in front of us, and Stafford and I completely missed it.

My father was very keen on me taking over Doug Laurie Sporting Goods Limited with my partners. Surprisingly, once we finally did, the store contained very little of the kind of stock that we wanted to sell. Harry and I prepared a list and ordered as much inventory as we could, hoping it would arrive for the busy Christmas shopping season. Many times, we'd go to sell a pair of new skates to a customer, only to pull down the box and find it filled with old, worn-out ones. With my trusting nature I assumed his staff had robbed poor Doug Laurie, but Harry said, "Tom, are you nuts? Forget poor Doug. It's you and me who bought empty boxes." When you're young and taking over a business, the learning curve is steep, and we definitely learned the hard way.

Our aim was to slowly make the evolution from selling sporting goods to Leaf souvenirs. We found a hot seller in custom Leaf jerseys; numbered and crested with the names of favourite players on the back. As business started to explode, Harold Ballard took notice, and gave us an eviction notice three weeks after Dad's funeral. The deal with Harold was "no lease, 30 days notice." He was within his rights, but his decision was in my opinion hardly fair. Addison panicked, certain that we'd be out of our location before Christmas. I went to King Clancy and asked if there was anyway he could intervene. "I'll handle it-don't worry. Stay quiet and I'll get back to you," Clancy said. And he did save our business. But Harold still refused to provide us with a lease.

It was a great Christmas season for us in 1971. Sales were outstanding, and by the time I locked the front door behind the last shopper on Christmas Eve, Harry and I collapsed into our chairs, exhausted, but excited with our exceptional sales. I went to the rack of custom Leaf sweaters, and counted that just nine remained. Our stock estimates had been almost exact, and we were convinced that with more time to get inventory next December, we'd do that much better. Sure enough, sales volumes the following December were five times higher than in our first six months.

Harry and I wished each other compliments of the season, and turned to enjoy our respective Christmases. As Harry bounced down Church Street, the building manager, Don "Shanty" MacKenzie, intercepted me before I reached the door. Shanty had served in World War II with Conn, and was rewarded upon his return with a job at Maple Leaf Gardens. He was embarrassed, but had a job to do and quietly said, "Tom, you and Harry have been evicted again. You have 30 days. I'm really sorry. I hope you can still have a merry Christmas."

My first wife Anne and I tucked our son Tommy into bed, telling him that when he woke up, Santa Claus would have come. Even though Tommy was just a toddler, he was as excited as any child could be. Anne was too, and excused herself to retire early. I hadn't said a word to anybody about the eviction, and wouldn't until Boxing Day. Instead, I sat in my big comfortable chair in front of the fire, watching the fire's glow and adding logs until 4:00 in the morning. My two dogs slept on the floor beside me. I could not stop thinking about how much I missed my father, and how much my life had changed.

On Boxing Day, I told Anne about the eviction notice. She put on a brave face in front of our son, but I knew she was as devastated as I. Once again, I called my old pal Clancy and told him the story. He rattled off 50 of the filthiest words known to mankind. Then said, "Forgive me Lord, I apologize. Try not to worry too much Tommy. I'll do the best I can for you and Harry."

While I was growing up, my neighbour was Ann Roper. I became good friends with Harry Addison Jr. in high school, and at one point, introduced him to Roper. They dated for years and eventually married. The four of us became great friends. My wife Anne and I went over to visit Harry and Ann that

Boxing Day. But it wasn't a typical Christmas visit: I had to break the news of the eviction. Harry was even more terrified this time than before. Harry finally told me he thought I should consider the buy-sell agreement. If I could put up with all these troubles, he'd step aside and I could buy him out of Doug Laurie's. But if I felt I couldn't handle the situation, he would buy me out. I knew that I couldn't walk away, and I sensed that Harry was not comfortable with the situation at the Gardens. I had been around the Gardens my entire life and knew the inner workings and the people associated so I decided to deal with the evictions alone and become the sole owner of Doug Laurie's. I was pleased when Harry said, "We are all too close as friends to let this store break us apart."

So there I was, at the dawning of 1972, owner of Doug Laurie's while I continued to manage the Toronto Marlboros — the whole chain, from the atoms all the way up to Junior. Eight teams in all. I was certainly busy, and knew what chronic fatigue felt like. From the time I was young, I had worked long hours. As a boy, I worked around the Gardens and helped Conn with his horses. During my teenage years, I helped Grandpa at the stables and also went on the scouting missions. Even before the Doug Laurie's opportunity came along, I was working at two jobs on a consistent basis. At 21, I was managing the Marlboros and working at General Motors' head office, where I oversaw the Pontiac Firebird and Corvette lines. A year or so later, I was hired away from GM by Wilson-Niblett Motors Limited in Richmond Hill, where I took care of new car deliveries. And I was still managing the Marlies. While at Wilson-Niblett, I used my experience from General Motors, and talked Gordon Wilson into carrying Corvettes. It wasn't long before Wilson-Niblett was the biggest Corvette dealer in Canada.

The 1971-72, Junior A Marlies were a talented and dedicated team. We challenged for the Memorial Cup once again and had boasted 14 sell-out games, incredible for junior hockey. In my back pocket, I knew I had Mark Howe joining his brother Marty on the Marlboros for 1972-73. If I could keep the nucleus of the team together, there was no stopping us. A few of the boys- including Dave Gardner, Bill Harris and Steve Shutt — would likely be first-round NHL draft choices that summer. And with each first-round pick came a $100,000.00 compensation cheque. The world looked bright, and by the end of June, the entire Marlboro team was signed for the following season. I was optimistic and felt it was now time to enjoy the summer. I drove up to Muskoka, relaxed and feeling great, and was all set for a good time in Ontario's beautiful cottage country with my family. We celebrated with a sunset cruise on my boat, slowly maneuvering through the calm, Maple Leaf blue water.

Chapter Twenty

It Was the Worst of Times, It Was the Best of Times

The loons usually rouse me from peaceful cottage sleeps. But on one July morning in 1972, it was the screams of my youngest sister Elizabeth. "Tommy, Tommy, Tommy," she wailed, trying to speak through her tears. "Read this!" She practically threw The Toronto Star at me. There it was: a story reporting that I had been fired. The article was very critical of my work. Neither Harold Ballard nor anyone else in the Marlboros management had ever previously discussed any of the issues detailed in the article with me. I also read that all of my personal belongings had been removed from my office and left in the public lobby. Twenty years of my life, sitting unceremoniously in the lobby-pictures, trophies, letters and souvenirs. By the time I got to Toronto, three-quarters of my belongings had been pilfered. How could Harold have done this to me? He'd been a second father to me for most of my life. Was it because the Marlboros had earned more than the Leafs in the prior few years? Was it because I was the last remaining link to the Smythes? Or was it because I was so much more involved in Maple Leaf Gardens than his sons? I don't think I'll ever know the real reason for my firing.

I returned to the cottage and sat there, all but comatose, for days. Ballard had named former Maple Leaf captain George Armstrong the new coach of the Marlboros. Frank Bonello was elevated from coach to general manager. And I was offered a position as assistant manager to Ray Miron with the Leafs' Central Hockey League affiliate, the Tulsa Oilers, which I declined. I had too many ties to Toronto and was not prepared to move away at that time. Anne and I had Tommy, still in diapers, and were expecting the birth of Christy. Mom needed me more than ever. She had become a widow just nine months before and was having a tough time learning to cope with life on her own. Besides, I still had Doug Laurie's, and didn't want to give that up for a move to a new city and uncertain future.

My mind was numb all summer. I could not let go of Maple Leaf Gardens after all those years, so I decided to hang on to Doug Laurie's instead, where I could at least be close by. King Clancy and I grew even closer. Twice more, Harold tried to have me evicted, and twice more, King stayed the executions. King told me to avoid Harold in the hallways, keep my profile low and watch what I said to everyone. The walls had ears when it came to Ballard. Troubled, I asked King, "How can you be so close to Harold after all that he's done?" His reply was profound. "Tommy m'boy, you're on the wrong track," he said. "It's not Harold my heart belongs to — it's Maple Leaf Gardens. And all the Stanley Cups we've won were won in part because of the Smythe family. Tommy, you and me, we're the same. We don't want to leave MLG until the day we die. That tells you everything you need to know. I'm here with you forever."

Avoiding Harold in the halls of Maple Leaf Gardens proved to he fairly easy. But when Harold had his heart problems, I swallowed my pride and went to visit him. Once, when he was in a Florida hospital, I visited him there, too. Clearly, Harold was surprised to see me, but he dropped the bravado and returned to man I knew as a child. Once his health improved and he returned to the Gardens, he'd pass by me in the hallways and not even respond to my "hellos."

Years later, on November 8, 1986, I was listening to the radio when I heard that Francis King Clancy had died of a heart attack at the age of 83. Great sadness enveloped me. King had been just like part of the Smythe family. He had been a fixture at Maple Leaf Gardens since 1930 when my grandfather traded two players and $35,000 to the Ottawa Senators for him in October of that year. Grandpa had won the money for the trade by betting on the horses and winning on a long shot named "Rare Jewel". King played six exceptional seasons for the Leafs, and retired in blue and white during his seventh. He later coached in the Toronto farm system, and joined the Leafs as coach in 1953-54, a position he held for three years. King was the assistant general manager for the better part of the rest of his life, and later returned behind the bench during the 1967 Stanley Cup playoff drive to replace Imlach during his hospitalization for exhaustion. He coached on an emergency basis again in 1971-72 when John McLellan fell ill with ulcer problems. Clancy had been a close friend to three generations of Smythes, but as much as I would miss him, I knew that the hockey world and the city of Toronto were also diminished significantly by his death.

Coming out of King's funeral, I heard a familiar voice call to me. "Hey Tommy!" It was Harold Ballard. "You're on your own, who's going to look after you now?" He laughed and walked away. His callousness hurt and disturbed me, and played havoc with my sleep for quite a while. When I finally could sleep, I often dreamed of King. Once I saw him looking down at me with a worried look on his face. I sat up, wide awake and struggled to see my alarm clock. It was just five in the morning, but I decided to get up anyway. The dream had given me a great idea.

I walked over to my desk and began to work on a rough draft of my idea, then phoned my lawyer, Bob Durno, at 7am and read it to him. "It's about time Tommy," Bob responded. "Good luck. I'll have it ready for you by the time you can get over here." I rushed over to Bob's office, picked up the proposal, and raced to the Hot Stove Lounge in Maple Leaf Gardens to catch Harold Ballard before he finished his breakfast.

Harold knew his health was declining, and had heart problems that reminded him of his mortality. Knowing that his time was ticking away, he had been working on a monstrous deal to sell Maple Leaf Gardens. There were three anxious groups ready to bid: The two largest Canadian breweries, Molson's, and Labatt's and Steve Stavro owner of a grocery chain and one of the Gardens' board of directors.

As I sat down in front of Harold at the table, I knew I was taking a calculated risk. "What the hell are you doing here so early? Get lost," he grumbled. I pulled out all my courage and started. "Good morning, Harold. I have a great idea that you are going to love." He cocked one eyebrow, glanced up at me and said, "Go ahead, but it better be good." After a quick swallow, I continued, "Look Harold, all the buyers are fighting hard to make a deal with you. What if they were faced with a 20-year lease on Doug Laurie's? They'd have to think twice about any ideas that they had for renovations or anything else." Harold lit up. "I love it, Tommy. Get the damn thing drawn up!"

I was just reaching into my suit jacket for the proposal when Harold's son Bill ran into the Hot Stove. "Dad. Don't listen to Tom," he insisted. But Harold wouldn't listen to Bill. "Get out of here Bill, and leave us alone," Harold barked. "And don't you ever tell me what to do again." I wasn't sure how Bill discovered my plan, but relieved when Ballard ignored his attempted intervention.

Harold took out his pen, and signed the papers that I had placed on the table. Deep down, I was practically in shock. Imagine Harold signing a lease for me, let alone one for 20 years. But I didn't want Harold to know how incredulous I was.

"Tommy, stop worrying now. I won't be around for long and I love the idea that the Gardens buyers will have to deal with this. That's a nice smile, Tommy. I'll see you later." And with that, Harold wiped his mouth and got up from the table. That was the last pleasant memory I have of a man who had been like a father to me for most of my life, and at other times, was my worst nightmare.

Before I was so dramatically fired from the Toronto Marlboros, I knew that the 1972-73 team I had helped assemble was outstanding, and it truly proved to be exactly that. The team lost only seven games during the regular season, finishing in first place with 103 points. Both Mark and Marty Howe were now playing on the team, and both had strong seasons. Mark, as a Marlboro rookie, scored 38 goals and had 104 points. My old pal Glenn Goldup scored 95 points. Wayne Dillon was sensational. He had accumulated 28 points in my last season with the team, but exploded for 107 scoring points in 1972-73, leading the team. Howe, Goldup and Dillon played on the same line, and their cumulative point total of 302 made many fans forget the line of Dave Gardner, Billy Harris and Steve Shutt. Rookie goaltender Mike Palmateer led the league with the best goals-against average, and was not only excellent in net, but also spectacular to watch because of his acrobatic moves. And the draft pick that had other teams laughing at me? Bob Dailey was now captain of the Marlboros.

The Marlies met second-place Peterborough Petes in the OHA final. The series went the full seven games, and the last game set a junior record for attendance by drawing a sell-out crowd of 16,485 to Maple Leaf Gardens. Toronto got past the Petes on a penalty shot goal by Paulin Bourdeleau with a minute left in the final game. The Marlboros earned the right to compete for the Memorial Cup in a round-robin tournament that pitted the champions of the three branches of junior hockey against each other. The Toronto Marlboro, winners of the Ontario Hockey

League, would be facing the Quebec Remparts of the Quebec Junior Hockey League and the Medicine Hat Tigers of the Western Hockey League.

All three teams were similarly talented and, after two games, each had won one game and lost another. The final was decided on goals for and against. In the deciding game, the Marlboros faced off against the Remparts. There was no contest. Toronto skated the Remparts into the ice with a lopsided 9-1 victory.

There were four special guests at that championship game. Gordie and Colleen Howe were there in Quebec to see their boys' victory. And Mom and I were in attendance too. We were sitting in the first row right behind the penalty box. When the Memorial Cup was presented to the Toronto Marlboros, Mark Howe skated the trophy over to the penalty box area and handed the trophy to Mom and me. It was a very emotional moment. The Marlboros acknowledged me for my contribution, which built that championship team.

Chapter Twenty-One

Courage

My Maple Leaf life was slowly drifting away, and I was undecided as to which way I should turn. It was my good friend John Blair who suggested a new career possibility. "Tom, you've always worked well with people, why don't you try real estate." He told me that he'd put in a favour with a friend at Johnston and Daniels Real Estate. I thought about if for a few weeks, then figured. "Why not? What have I got to lose?" I had no idea that I was opening the door to a new life.

It had been years since I'd been in school, and had to redevelop myself to study and prepare for exams. My life had been hockey, hockey and more hockey. Now, suddenly, I was embracing new knowledge and a new culture. As the three months of preparation evaporated, I grew more excited and, before I knew it, I'd written the exam. I did well, and was hired on by Jamie Gairdner, as the new realtor at Johnston and Daniels Real Estate.

Because I had grown up in the west end of Toronto, I started at the company's Kingsway office. The early months were slow, but as I gained confidence, my sales escalated. By the end of my first year, I was a Diamond Award winner — indicating annual sales in excess of $1.5 million. By my third year, I found that my hockey connections led me to more listings and sales in the downtown core, so I made the decision to relocate to the central office on Mount Pleasant.

My first day there, the manager, led me up the stairs to show me my office. I unpacked my belongings and set up my desk. I hung a few hockey pictures on the wall and erected two desk lamps. When my new office partner Penny entered, she looked shocked and commented that she had never seen the office so tidy or neatly decorated. She sat down, turned her chair in my direction, and said. "Don't ever smoke or touch my papers. Don't listen to my phone conversations and don't ever wear cologne of any kind." "Wow," I thought. "Great start." We didn't speak much to each other for the next two years, but we eventually became casual friends.

I applied the same energy and commitment to my real estate career as I had used to become a success in hockey. But besides selling real estate, I was still working at Doug Laurie's on game nights and Saturdays. The pressures at home started to mount. My wife Anne was interested in the more glamorous side of our life — attending charity fund-raising dinners, fashion shows, and our membership at private clubs. I have never been shy about supporting charities, but was uninterested with high society. Anne and I were living beyond our means, and the expenses were starting to choke me. I was, however, too proud to say anything to Anne. I convinced myself that things would rectify themselves. Our children, Tommy and Christy, were in school, and I didn't want to alarm them either. And amidst all the economic and time pressures, the Maple Leaf Gardens fiasco still lingered in my head.

My candle was burning down at both ends. Many days, I'd drive from home in Etobicoke to downtown Toronto, return to Etobicoke in the evening, then drive back downtown to Doug Laurie's. I missed time with my children and often woke them up when I returned home around midnight, only so I could hold them and rock them back to sleep. Tommy and Christy are adults now, but the feelings haven't changed.

Anne and I had long conversations about moving out of Etobicoke into downtown Toronto. It made sense as far as my job went, and it would put us closer to Branksome Hall, Christy's school. Unbeknownst to Anne, it was also my chance to scale down our economic situation. We purchased a condominium that was one-third of a monstrous heritage mansion near Sherbourne North and Maple in the Rosedale area of downtown Toronto. When it was built, homeowners weren't allowed to have stables near the house, and this beautiful home had a tunnel that led down to where the stables would have been kept, which is now scenic Rosedale Valley. The house was incredible, but undergoing renovations so by the time we moved from our home on North Drive in Etobicoke, we were forced to rent for several months.

Moving day, brought excitement to the rest of the family, but I still carried the burden of my worries. Our new home was a very reasonable size, and had a gas fireplace, so on those many nights when I couldn't sleep; I wouldn't have to feed logs to the fire. Even though I had tried to reduce my debt load, I was right back where I had been; struggling with a large mortgage, bank loans and the worries of a relationship that was starting to unravel.

Anne and I and the kids had two beloved family pets, Peanut and Shannon. Shannon was an Irish Setter who was forever running away. We often found him prancing through the neighbourhood drenched to the bone. Shannon frequently took the liberty of going for a swim in neighbours' pools. As time went on, Shannon disappeared for entire days. Finally, a lady called us. "Hi Mr. Smythe? I've got your beautiful Irish Setter over here, and I got your phone number off his collar. I hesitated calling you, but your dog is over at my house every day. He's well-behaved, with such a sweet disposition, and my son just loves him, but I thought you must be worried." I was, and went over to get Shannon, not all that far from where we lived. When I got there, I got a lump in my throat. There was Shannon alright, his head in the lap of the lady's son; a young boy in a wheelchair. They were clearly great friends, and Shannon was very protective of his new pal. I decided that while my family was away during the day, we would leave Shannon with this young boy. He was ecstatic with this arrangement and looked forward to greeting Shannon each morning.

Our new home had a big antique fireplace. It hadn't been used for years, but I just knew that families through the years must have enjoyed sitting in front of the beautiful hearth. We had it converted to gas. When we moved in, no one enjoyed being in front of that fireplace more than Shannon. When I came home from work, I'd usually find the fireplace turned on, and the Irish Setter lying happily in front of it. I never thought much about it, except the fireplace would be on in warm weather too. "Come on kids," I scolded Tommy and Christy, "The dog doesn't need to have the fireplace on every day of the year." They were visibly upset. "Dad, we didn't touch the fireplace," they responded. "Right. Then I guess he just turns it on by himself," I sarcastically concluded.

I came home a little early one day, and walked through the living room. Sure enough, there was Shannon, over at the baseboard where the "on-off" switch was located, pushing it on with his nose. Darned dog Shannon was too smart for his own good, and too expensive for my gas bill.

The Christmas season was approaching and in order to lighten our spirit's, Anne and I decided to host a cocktail party. It was Christmas Eve and we cordially welcomed our many friends, family and co-workers, including the agent who sold us our condo mansion — my office partner Penny.

The following year, Christmas Eve 1986, Anne and I hosted another party. In addition to all our friends and co-workers, virtually every member of the Smythe family would be there. As Anne and I made last-minute adjustments, she reached over to give me a kiss. As she took my face into her hands, she recoiled quickly. "Tom, what's this? There's a bump just behind your ear." "Let's get Uncle Hugh to take a look." "Anne, slow down," I responded." It's Christmas Eve and I'll get it checked later." But Anne wouldn't hear of it, and when my Dad's brother, Dr. Hugh Smythe arrived, he took a closer look. Hugh seemed concerned and insisted I make alternate plans for Christmas morning. "Meet me in my hospital office tomorrow, Tom," he said. "I'll have Dr. Simon McGrail with me. He's an ear, nose and throat specialist."

Sleep refused to come that night. My mind was plagued with thoughts of Maple Leaf Gardens and all the bills that were piling up. Now this. I tossed and turned. I'm not certain that I got any sleep, but the next thing I knew, Tommy and Christy were up and ready to open their gifts. By the time the last present was unwrapped and we had finished Christmas breakfast, it was 10 o'clock. I slipped out of the house and made my way to my uncle's office. My life would never be the same.

Dr. McGrail examined all around my left ear, fingering the bump over and over. "Tom, you've got a cyst, but I don't think it's cancerous," the doctor explained.

Surgery was scheduled for a few weeks following. Dr. McGrail explained that there was a risk that a nerve may either be pushed or enclosed by the cyst. If that was the case, he would try to remove the cyst in pieces to preserve the nerve. As my stretcher was rolled towards the operating room, a nurse asked me to remove all jewelry, including my dad's Stanley Cup ring. "There is no way I'll take off this ring," I said. "But Mr. Smythe," the nurse countered, "it's a hospital rule." "Okay then," I continued, "Turn this bed around and I'll go get dressed. I'm not taking this ring off." Finally, she conceded that this was an argument she was never going to win, so she taped the ring to my finger. For every one of my many operations, it's been the same procedure. After a while, they didn't even ask; they'd just pull out the adhesive tape.

All Stanley Cup rings are incredible, but my father's is a little different. Whenever I show it to people, their eyes dance and they break into a huge smile. Robert Amell and Company designed the Stanley Cup rings worn by the victorious Leafs of the sixties. Jack Amell, vice-president of the company, was Dad's good friend, a member of the Silver Seven hockey committee and Conn's next-door neighbour at the cottage. The original ring for the 1961-62 victory was beautiful, and had a small diamond in the centre. With each subsequent Stanley Cup victory, the diamond in the centre was replaced by a larger one. Because my Dad won four Stanley Cups, the diamond is now close to two carats. On the left side, there's an embossed Stanley Cup; on the right, the years of the Stanley Cup victories. There are fewer than 20 people who own a ring exactly like this one, and they are the players, staff and management of the Toronto Maple Leafs who played on each of the four Stanley Cup winning teams in the 1960s: George Armstrong, Bob Baun, Johnny Bower, Tim Horton, Larry Hillman, Red Kelly, Dave Keon, Frank Mahovlich, Bob Pulford, Eddie Shack, Allan Stanley, plus coach and general manager Punch Imlach, trainer Bob Haggert and, of course, Harold Ballard and Stafford Smythe.

I glance at the ring every day, and remember that the night before Dad died, his watch and ring were removed by the hospital staff and left on the night table, ignored. Thirty-one hours later, my Uncle remembered the jewelry and rushed back to the room, where it sat untouched. Uncle Hugh retained my dad's watch as a memory of his brother and I took possession of Dad's ring.

There are some peculiar things about my father's Stanley Cup ring. Even though the ring has had a tremendous amount of wear, the engraving of my father's name is still clearly evident on the inside. For inspiration and strength, I rub the left side where the Stanley Cup is displayed. On occasion, I've rubbed the ring's Stanley Cup when I wanted the Leafs to win a game or score a pivotal goal. As childish as it sounds, the little ritual has helped. Yet the Stanley Cup has never worn away. Having said that, I have never touched the right side where the years of the Stanley Cup victories are displayed, and that side has completely vanished. When my father is rightfully voted into the Hockey Hall of Fame, I will have that right side re-engraved.

After my first six-hour operation, I recuperated in my hospital bed for several days. On the third morning, Dr. McGrail came into my room and, with a somber look, asked all my visitors to leave the room. I was in pain and had asked to keep the curtains drawn. When Dr. McGrail closed the door, it made the room very dark. "Tom," he began, "You've got a very rare form of cancer. I don't know how to tell you this, so I'm just going to come right out and say that you likely have only one to three years to live." I fell into shock. My initial reaction was, "No tears — I'm going to fight this battle and win." My hand fumbled for Dad's ring, and I rubbed the left side. My grandfather's favourite expression was, "If you can't beat 'em in the alley, you can't beat 'em on the ice." I reworked the saying as I lay there: "If you can't beat 'em in the hospital, you can't continue to live your life." At that moment, my daughter Christy came into the room with tears in her eyes. She handed me a small note. It was a teenage girl's expression of love to her father. As I read it, the tears poured down my cheeks. I continue to carry it in my wallet, and whenever I need extra reassurance, I read it again.

Dr. Simon McGrail informed me that I was only the 61st patient in the twentieth century to be diagnosed with Adenocystic Carcinoma of the Parodit. This is a rare and unpredictable cancer that attacked oddly enough my main saliva gland. Just before the third operation, Dr. McGrail introduced me to a new intern in Toronto from Ireland, Dr. Peter Neligan. In his Irish brogue, he told me, "If you lined up a hundred doctors from anywhere in the world, I'd be willing to bet that no more than three would recognize the name of this cancer, let alone know what to do to help you, Tom." We both agreed that if I wasn't aggressive in fighting this disease, I would have no hope of beating it. Between my hockey experiences and Irish Smythe blood coursing through my veins, I knew what fighting was all about, and there was no way I was going to go down without the battle of my life — literally and figuratively.

Since 1986, my medical chart details 31 operations, 52 radiation treatments, a tracheotomy, more X-rays than the Leafs have pucks, CAT scans, MRI scans, bone scans, 60 hyperbaric chamber treatments and literally thousands of blood tests. Then, there are the tougher parts to reveal — three failed operations, one slight stroke plus my life written off three different times. I have grown incredibly close to my amazing doctors: Doctors McGrail, Neligan, Gullane, Bradley, Evans, Cummings and Thomas.

In 1992, I learned self-hypnosis. This ability allowed me to focus and ease the tension in parts of my body. In the midst of preparing for an 18-hour facial operation in 1994, I decided to put my new ability to work. Both Dr. Peter Neligan and his partner, Dr. Pat Gullane have fabulous senses of humour, so I decided to make them a bet. "Peter? Pat? You feel like making a little wager?" They responded, "Let's hear it first." "Okay," I continued, "If I can lose less than 10 ounces of blood during this operation, the two of you and your wives are taking Penny and I for dinner, at the restaurant of my choice, anywhere in Ontario. You guys in?" The doctors laughed, "You're on, Tom!" Eighteen hours later, I began to regain consciousness from the anesthetic. I struggled to open my eyes, and when I did, the world looked like it was cloaked in a cloud. As my eyes began to adjust, I saw doctors and nurses ringing my bed and thought to myself, "Oh, shit, this doesn't look good, I must be in big trouble." When I finally came to, I isolated Drs. Neligan and Gullane from the crowd. "How'd I do?" I asked cautiously, terrified of the answer. Neligan was quick to answer, "You did great Tommy." He then brought up his hand clutching a paper cup from behind his back. "Four ounces, Tom. We only used two sponges. Congratulations — where do you want to go for dinner?"

As I remained in the hospital, my good friends Dick Duff, Darryl Sittler, George Armstrong and Johnny Bower visited me. My Leaf pals hadn't forgotten me. "Tommy, we're all saying our prayers for you," I realized more than ever that the Toronto Maple Leafs would always be with me. Leaf alumni continued to visit me throughout the year and all the ones following.

As I was going through my cancer treatments, I popped into St. Michael's Cathedral in downtown Toronto one day to listen to Mass. My mind drifted back to my childhood, and my many memories. I started to think about Gibby-Toes. That was the nickname we kids had for my grandmother Rose Gaudette, my mother's mom. Where the name "Gibby-Toes" originated is a mystery.

From the time I was four until I turned 12, our family spent summers at Orchard Beach on Lake Simcoe. Gibby-Toes would come up too, and each day, she and I would talk non-stop, chatting about virtually everything. Our conversations quite often focused on religion. Gibby-Toes was a devout Roman Catholic. She had endured a tough life, having lost her husband when she was 38 years old. After Mom and Dad married, we were raised Anglican, but I had a lot of questions about my grandmother's religion. She answered every question, no matter how complex or naive, with the same positive attitude she approached everything.

Rose Gaudette boarded Toronto Marlboro Junior players at her home. Many of the boys were from outside of Toronto, and being away from home for the first time was difficult for many. Gibby-Toes made them feel like they were at a home away from home. Often I would visit my grandmother's house, and the hockey players would treat me like a little brother. In fact, I was taught to skate at the age of three by Toronto Marlboro players

George Armstrong and Mike Nykoluk. Armstrong went on to play his entire 20-season career with the Leafs, starting in 1949-50 and retiring after the 1970-71 season. He later coached the Marlboros to two Memorial Cup championships, and was named coach of the Leafs for part of the 1988-89 season. Nykoluk played half a season on right wing with Toronto in 1956-57, and later returned to coach the Leafs between 1981 and 1984.

When Gibby-Toes died, I spoke at her funeral. There I stood, at the front of Our Lady of Perpetual Sorrows Cathedral on Bloor Street West in Etobicoke, not far from our family home. For a lady who mourned her husband's death for the remainder of her own life, it was an ironic name for the church where she was to be bid farewell. It took me a minute to gain my composure, but once I did, I spoke for 20 minutes. The priest thought I would go on forever, and he looked at me with that "that's fine, thank you, now find your seat" sort of look. But I spoke until I had said everything I felt.

The second time I visited St. Michael's Cathedral; I stopped to light a candle for Gibby-Toes and another one for my father. Monsignor Ken Robitaille walked over and greeted me. "Hello there, Tom Smythe. I know you from Maple Leaf Gardens. I have relatives who play in the NHL. You may have heard of Luc Robitaille." I said hello and shook his hand. He mentioned that I appeared saddened and offered his time if I wanted to talk.

I later returned to St. Mike's and spent a great deal of time with the Monsignor, unburdening myself as I spoke of my operations, the impact of losing Conn and Irene, Rose and Dad, plus the loss of my chance to run the Toronto Maple Leafs. Over the course of several months, our meetings occurred with greater frequency, and I grew to acknowledge that I had found a new friend. Monsignor Robitaille, I told him one day, "you have done me more good than you'll ever know." I then asked whether he would receive me into his church. He agreed and on the day I was made a Roman Catholic I swear I saw Rose

Gaudette at the back of the cathedral. I blinked in disbelief, but when I opened my eyes, she was gone.

I laugh when I think what Conn would have said if I could tell him I converted to Catholicism. He had given Dad and Mom such a hard time over their inter-denominational marriage. But as tough as Conn was, he also had a great heart, and I'm certain that if he was with me today, he'd find out how peaceful and happy my adopted religion has made me.

My first experience with radiation was with Dr. Cummings at Princess Margaret Hospital in Toronto. He explained the process and asked if I was interested to see the radiation equipment. We left his office and walked down to the treatment room. "Right in here, Tom," Dr. Cummings pointed. I froze in my tracks. The room number was 13. I informed him that there was no way I'd have any treatment in a room numbered such as this. He acknowledged my concern and said, "Tom, I've got an idea. By the time you show up for your appointment tomorrow morning and I'll have it taken care of." The next morning at nine, I arrived for my treatment, curious about how Cummings handled the situation. As I walked along the hall, I took a concerted look at the numbers above the doorframes. Sure enough, Dr. Cummings was good for his word. The radiation room was now 12A. I couldn't help but chuckle, thinking about the doctor's ingenuity.

To get myself through the treatments, I brought a picture of the Grand Hotel used for the filming of the movie, Somewhere in Time, along with me. I would stare at it during the radiation, thinking that when this all was over, I would travel there for a well-deserved holiday. It was February and I vowed that by August I would be standing on that magnificent porch, alive and well.

Radiation wasn't easy, but on August 1, I walked up the steps of the Grand Hotel of Macinaw Island's mansion. I laboured a little, but once I reached the porch, I turned around and faced a spectacular sight. Just past the lighthouse, Lakes Michigan and Huron merge. The sun was brilliant, and I had to squint to see the sailboats on the horizon. I had made it. Pillar to pillar, I glance back at the horizon, my eyes moist with tears of joy, and marvel that I was there at all. The porch seemed to extend forever. Whenever I feel down, I reach into my memory of that August day and my spirit soars. I have truly learned to treasure each day as though it might be my last. There were many days when it almost was.

Chapter Twenty-Two

Major

I could really see Grandpa's health starting to deteriorate in 1980, during which time I made an effort to spend more and more time with him. Conn knew that his time was nearing an end, and he looked forward to my visits. He loved to regale me with stories about his marvelous life.

Many of the stories revolved around World War II. Great Britain declared war on Germany in September 1939. Canada followed suit within days, and by December of that year, the first Canadian troops had landed in Europe. My grandfather, the proud Canadian that he was, attempted to enlist immediately, in spite of the fact he was 44 years old and a father of three. Conn had already served in World War I, where he earned a Military Cross. My grandmother tried to keep Conn from enlisting again, but to no avail. When he was turned down because of his age, Grandpa went down to the old Woodbine Racetrack and tried to force the hand of the Armed Forces by forming a Sportsmen's Battalion. Men with sports backgrounds were encouraged to enlist-lacrosse players, golfers, football and hockey players and even sportswriters joined. By September 1941, Conn was finally able to convince the Army to sanction his battalion, and the 30th Battery of the Canadian Active Army was formed, with Major Constantine Falkland Cary Smythe in command.

Major Smythe wrote letters to each of the Toronto Maple Leafs players, farmhands and off-ice employees, urging them to enlist in the war effort as quickly as possible. My grandfather felt that these men should receive their training right away, so that if they were called upon to serve their country, they would be ready. The response from the Leaf organization was overwhelming; a source of pride to my grandfather to the end of his life. Twenty-two Maple Leaf regulars and minor leaguers interrupted their careers to enlist. Syl Apps, Turk Broda, Pete Langelle, Bud Poile, Sweeney Schriner, Wally Stanowski, Gaye Stewart and Billy Taylor were Leaf stars who joined the Canadian Armed Forces. Don Metz signed up for the Royal Canadian Air Force. Bob Goldham, Joe Klukay and Gus Mortson entered the Royal Canadian Navy.

Conn spent more than 20 months in England, preparing his battery for the day they'd be called into battle. Then, shortly after the June 6, 1944, invasion of Normandy, Conn received orders that his battery would be next to invade. They waterproofed the artillery and packed the gear, and then it was only a matter of waiting the two or three days until the ship was ready to sail to France.

With the equipment packed, Conn and the troops decided to play some softball to pass the time. Grandpa told me how he almost didn't make it to the battlegrounds. A private named Joe Dwyer hit a double with no men out. The next batter pounded the ball, hitting the ground just in front of the plate and bouncing high and hard to Conn at third base. Grandpa fielded the ball cleanly and cocked his arm to fake a throw to first for the out, hoping to tag the advancing base runner. Dwyer read the play as Grandpa expected, and took off for third, where Conn was now crouched, cradling the ball in both hands and blocking the bag for the tag. Dwyer had no choice, and went hard into my grandfather, knowing that his only hope for avoiding the tag was to jar the ball loose from Conn's glove. Even though Joe Dwyer was a private and Conn an officer, he hit Grandpa with a shoulder that knocked him head over heels and left him unconscious. When he was revived, Conn was in terrible pain and finding it difficult to breathe. Someone yelled, "Get him to the hospital," but Conn wouldn't hear of it, knowing that the Army's medical staff would prohibit his accompanying the troops on the invasion. Grandpa was sure he had broken his ribs at the very least, so when one of the soldiers pulled up in a truck and said he'd find Grandpa a civilian doctor, Conn consented. The doctor verified my grandfather's diagnosis, and taped the ribs tightly. They put him in a private hospital and Conn, as stubborn and proud as anyone who ever existed, called his friend Ted Reeve, a Toronto newspaper reporter serving in Conn's battery, and ballplayer, Joe Dwyer, into the hospital room. "Look you guys, I am going to Normandy, and I don't care what anyone says," Conn wheezed. "If they send me home because I hurt myself in a ballgame, I'll never live it down. There's no way that's going to happen, so I want to make sure everyone keeps quiet. You got it?" Reeve nodded yes, Dwyer begged forgiveness. Conn extended his hand and replied, "No hard feelings, Private. I've nailed you a few times in other ways, and I guess one good turn deserves another."

Although it was supposed to be a secret, the commanding officers eventually discovered Conn's injury and tried to prohibit my grandfather from going to France. But Conn convinced them that after waiting almost two years, some sore ribs weren't going to stop him. Conn was strapped to a seat in the cab of a gun wagon and a crane swung the vehicle out over the French coast. The British Navy covered their arrival, hidden from sight behind them. Once Conn and the troops had emptied from the ship, they began their trek to Caen, a destination a few miles inland to the south. The road had been cleared a few days earlier right to the Orne River, where my grandfather's troops were to protect two bridges. The soldiers were aghast when they saw the devastation left behind by the German soldiers. Within hours, the German Air Force attacked Conn's battery, and several soldiers were wounded. Conn and his men set up their headquarters in a residence near the bridges.

It was July 18, and the fighting was fierce. The battle lasted two days, and the Allies suffered heavy casualties. Conn was still in pain and his breathing was laboured from the broken ribs. On July 25, the doctor finally took the tape from his side, and Conn found his breathing was much improved. That night under cover of darkness, the Germans attacked the bridges. Monstrous flares were dropped by parachute, lighting up the entire area. The gunfire was so insistent that the soldiers soon grew deaf to it. Bombs fell all around, spraying a vast area with fragments. Conn and his gunners began to run outside when my grandfather stopped and returned to camp to grab his heavy trench coat. What caused such an impulse, especially in light of the evening's heat, Conn never understood. When he stepped back outside, the fighting was ferocious. Everywhere he turned, Conn could see fires and explosions. His ears were rocked with the horrifying sounds of screams. Conn dashed over to an ammunition truck whose tarpaulin covering had caught fire. As he climbed up onto the truck, Grandpa was hit in the back with a terrific force. There was so much confusion and commotion that he never knew whether it was the truck's cargo exploding, or a bomb fragment from one of the many explosions. The blast threw my grandfather to the ground, where he lay near the headquarters. Grandpa tried to move, but couldn't. He seemed paralyzed from the waist down. Helpless, he lay there in intense pain, the bombs and gunfire continuing to explode all around him. Grandpa reached around to find the origin of his pain. His fingers touched a jagged piece of hot metal, still protruding from his back. The thickness of his heavy canvas trench coat had likely saved his life.

My grandfather laid there in that spot, unable to move, waiting for help to arrive. While gunfire and explosions went off all around him, he drifted far away from the war and thought about how his wife Irene had argued with him over his enlisting. He thought about how the commanding officers had tried to prevent him from serving. He thought about how the baseball injury had almost precluded his active duty. Yet there he was, in defiance of all those around him, lying on a French battlefield with a hunk of metal screaming out of his back. Conn's thoughts focused on a phrase his own father had instilled into his memory: "Each man is his own absolute law giver and the dispenser of glory or gloom to himself; the maker of his life, his reward, his punishment." This is one of the doctrines of the Theosophical Society, to which Conn's father — and later, Conn — belonged. The Society's beliefs are based on Hindu and Buddhist philosophy, centred around the thought that your lot in this life stems from your behavior in a previous life. My grandfather realized that what had occurred that horrific night was his own fate. He had forged his own destiny, but he always thanked a Higher Power for sending him back to get that trench coat.

When help finally arrived, Grandpa was shuttled to the Canadian casualty clearing station. The doctor attending asked, "Who is this one?" "Major Conn Smythe," came the reply. The doctor raised his head: "Wait a minute-The Connie Smythe from the Toronto Maple Leafs?" "Yes, one and the same," confirmed my grandfather. "Well then," said the doctor, "we certainly can't lose you now, can we?" Although most of the shrapnel was removed from my grandfather's back, they were never able to remove the entire piece of metal, as it was too close to his spine.

Conn was taken to a hospital in Basingstoke, and spent long, arduous days there. The arrival of correspondence was what he most looked forward to each day. My grandmother wrote religiously, and letters also arrived from Hap Day and Frank Selke. Hap was running C. Smythe For Sand while Conn was overseas, as well as acting as his eyes and ears on hockey matters. But more than Selke's letters dealing with the Gardens, it was the little printed letters from his daughter Patricia that Grandpa enjoyed the most. My father, Stafford, went to visit Conn in the British hospital while on leave. They almost had to admit him too, because he fainted the second he saw his father hooked up to all those tubes and bags.

Conn would never fully recover. His back would always cause him trouble, and his legs pained him for the rest of his life. A nerve in Grandpa's right leg had been cut, and it caused his toes to curl under, making walking painful. The shrapnel had also damaged my grandfather's bladder and bowels. This was initially something that my grandfather spoke of with great shame, but eventually, he accepted that there was no choice, and he would actually kid about it.

When he was well enough, Conn was carried to the ship Lady Nelson, and along with 500 other injured soldiers, set sail for Canada. They docked in Halifax on September 16 that year. Eventually, Grandpa arrived at Chorley Park Military Hospital, in Toronto's Rosedale area. Prior to being a hospital, it had once been the official residence of Ontario's Lieutenant Governor.

Grandpa had seen the war up close, and from his hospital bed, he railed at the government for sending poorly trained or inexperienced troops into battle. No shrinking violet, Conn was very vocal about the large numbers of unnecessary casualties, and he challenged Prime Minister William Lyon Mackenzie King and his Liberal government to do something about the Canadian soldiers, ill prepared for war. He also was adamant that there were too few reinforcements being sent into the European battle, and with under-manned troops came further casualties. My grandfather took his opinions to the press where he engaged in his own all-out war. The Toronto newspapers took differing sides on the reinforcement issue, and there was talk of a court martial for Conn because of his pointed accusations. The court martial never happened, and my grandfather always contended it was because the government knew he was right in his assertions. Grandpa asked to be discharged from the Army. His request was granted.

As the autumn hit Toronto, Grandpa was released to his home at 68 Baby Point. Irene took care of Conn with substantial help from Jessie Watson. Jessie had joined the Smythe family in 1931 to help with household duties. She was just 18 then, and she stayed with the family until Conn's death. Jessie was a delightful woman. My Dad often told us how Jessie had stayed up with him late into those nights when he'd suffer from an especially bad asthma attack.

Conn kept up with the Leafs from his bed, listening to Foster Hewitt's play-by-play on the radio and performing his day-to-day duties by telephone. He wasn't yet well enough to venture down to the Gardens. The Maple Leafs finished in third place during the 1944-45 season, but beat first-place Montreal in the semi-finals, then Detroit Red Wings in the finals to win the Stanley Cup. The Major had returned from the war to watch his team triumph as world champions.

During that season after Grandpa's return, a battle for power was being waged behind Conn's back. Some members of the Leaf executive felt that the organization could be better run without Conn's leadership. Frank Selke, who had been overseeing the Leaf operation in Grandpa's absence, was in pursuit of Grandpa's managing director position, and along with some key executives, he was intending to oust Conn.

One ploy was to suggest that Conn would be an appropriate choice as president of the NHL. The former President, Frank Calder, had passed away in 1943. When the New York Americans put their operation on hold, team president Mervyn Red Dutton was appointed the NHL president on an interim basis. Selke and his supporters suggested that Conn Smythe would be perfect for the job; a move which would have opened the presidency of the Toronto Maple Leafs for Selke. But my grandfather closed that discussion as quickly as it started. Not only would he not take on the NHL presidency, he helped convince Red Dutton to stay on in a permanent capacity.

Several members of the Gardens board of directors were divided in their loyalties. Selke had found support from Ed Bickle and Bill MacBrien. Conn had Jack Bickell and Percy Gardiner on his side. In fact, when Gardiner, who was a stockbroker, heard about the possible Selke takeover, he called my grandfather "Conn," he began, "You built the Gardens, and you built this organization into what it is today. But you'll need a lot more stock in order to control the Gardens. If you don't control more of the shares, every year there is the potential for a takeover. If I sell you my shares at fair market value, it'll give you 30,000 more, and that will give you control so you never have to go through this again." Grandpa was clearly taken aback at the show of support Gardiner was offering, but the money required for the purchase was far more than he had. Conn replied, "Percy, that is a fine offer and I thank you sincerely. But the shares are trading at about $10, so for me to buy your shares, I'd need $300,000, and I just don't have anywhere near that kind of money." Gardiner closed the sale. "Pay me what you can and the rest we'll carry over whatever time you need. When you win another Stanley Cup, or if you ever beat me at the racetrack, we can settle up then."

That's where Conn got the block of shares that enabled him to keep his presidency of Maple Leaf Gardens for as long as he wanted. Most hockey fans believed my grandfather had control of the Toronto Maple Leafs from day one, but it was not until 1947 that he truly gained control.

In 1964, Maple Leaf Gardens donated the Conn Smythe Trophy to the NHL to honour their founder. It's a magnificent trophy with a silver-plated miniature version of Maple Leaf Gardens dwarfed by a large silver maple leaf, all on a walnut base. The prize is awarded to the most valuable player in the Stanley Cup playoffs, selected at the conclusion of the last game of the finals by the Professional Hockey Writers' Association. The president of the NHL makes the presentation to the winner at centre ice just before the Stanley Cup is awarded to the winning team. My grandfather was thrilled with this honour. The recipients of the trophy have exemplified his fighting spirit. The first was the Canadiens' captain Jean Beliveau who led his team to the Stanley Cup that year. After Grandpa's death in 1980, the beautiful trophy was renamed the Conn Smythe Memorial Trophy.

My grandfather enjoyed another honour when the NHL introduced new names for the divisional competition within the league. Beginning with the 1974-75 season, the Smythe Division was one of two in the Campbell Conference. These divisional names were discontinued after the 1992-93 season.

In spite of his gruff exterior, my grandfather was a very kind and gentle man. Because of his proximity to death during World War II, combined with the loss of his darling Patricia, Conn got heavily involved in charitable work, especially those that involved children with physical challenges. After returning from the Second World War, Reg Hopper, a friend of Conn's from Jarvis Collegiate, asked him to join the Ontario Society for Crippled Children. This was the perfect opportunity for Conn to give something back to a society that had been very good to him and his family, while acknowledging Patricia and his own mobility challenges stemming from the war wound. Grandpa agreed, and was a lifelong board member and contributor. Each year, the Easter Seals Society (as it was renamed) hosts a charity event called the Conn Smythe Sports Celebrity Dinner, and raises hundreds of thousands of dollars in aid of children with physical and mental challenges.

In 1949, Conn was involved in securing a parcel of land at the junction of Kingston Road and Danforth in Scarborough for one dollar. This prime location was used by the Ontario Society for Crippled Children, in tandem with the Variety Club, to build a facility that would help children with mental and physical challenges to become self sufficient. The facility was named Variety Village, and continues to do marvelous work with youngsters.

Through these, the legacy of Conn Smythe is destined to live on for generations to come.

Chapter Twenty-Three

Coincidences in Time

My grandfather was weakening rapidly, and his storytelling had covered the better part of his life. All of his war stories reconfirmed how little my generation truly knows about the efforts those brave women and men like him had made to keep our country free. When I saw Spielberg's movie, "Saving Private Ryan," I couldn't help but reflect on the tales that Grandpa told me. One night when I went to visit him, he had a surprise for me. It was the ornate English sword he carried through both Great Wars. I treasure this artifact from my grandfather more than anything else I possess. At Conn's funeral, my son Tommy carried his great-grandfather's sword in respect of the Smythe name. It fills me with pride that I share the same bloodline with this incredible man.

Conn wanted to have his affairs in order for the inevitable. We spoke at length about his will. He insisted that those who had helped him throughout his life would be taken care of. There were some changes he wanted made though. One was that he didn't feel I needed the pressure of operating his stable of racehorses, and that he wanted me to sell them. He also wanted me to take care of those employees who helped with the horses. Conn and I chatted about how and where to sell his stable of 65, and we put it in writing as part of the will. The changes to the will were made within the week, and I promised Conn that I would always do my best for him, Irene, Patricia, Stafford and all his soldiers. That made him smile.

We used to call Grandpa's nurse "Meg," but her real name was Margaret Grose. Meg had looked after Irene in her final years, and had remained close to the family. When Conn's health started to fail, she asked him if he needed a full-time nurse, and said that she would very much like to take that role. In the late 1960s, Meg became Conn's live-in nurse at the house on Baby Point. While he definitely required daily medical assistance, he equally appreciated the companionship that both Meg and Jessie provided. Both accompanied him on outings, and the three had a grand time going to Woodbine Racetrack and Maple Leaf Gardens together.

One morning when I was in my office, the phone rang. It was a distraught Meg screaming, "Tom, Tom — urgent. Get over here as fast as you can." I raced, screeching the car into the Baby Point driveway and rushed up the stairs to Grandpa's bedroom. My grandfather was unconscious. Kneeling beside the bed, I took his hand and whispered, "It's time to let go Grandpa." I felt Conn squeeze my hand. "Turn your head and look at the front window Grandpa. Irene is waiting for you." Again, Conn squeezed my hand, then smiled and though unconscious, turned his head to the window. At that second, I could feel Grandpa's spirit leave his body. I have thought about heaven a lot in my life, but I have never experienced such a powerful, more intimate moment. I glanced at the clock on Conn's nightstand. It read 11:11.

After Conn died, Christie's, the world-famous auction company was brought in to sell my grandfather's furnishings and personal effects. I went over to the house one day, to find all of Conn's furniture out on the front lawn. If I have but one regret concerning material items, it's that I didn't ask for Conn's beautiful antique grandfather clock. It would have been symbolic for me to own my grandfather's grandfather clock, especially considering how important time has become to me.

My father's death occurred at 4:44. Conn died at 11:11. It made me wonder whether coincidences are really just random events with common ties, or parts of a larger picture. I was convinced that both my father and grandfather let me know that they're observing my life by presenting me with a common thread between important events. Some might call them coincidences, but I prefer to consider them mini-miracles.

Shortly after my grandfather's death I was at home thinking of him when my phone rang. I picked it up as usual. "Hello?" "Hi Tom. This is George Gardiner. Hey, remember you told me you were concerned about having to sell Conn's racehorses? Well, I'd like to help." I stammered some answer, and let him continue. "My recommendation is that we get three evaluations from different horse centres, let's say Kentucky, London, England and Toronto. I'll average the three amounts and add 20 percent. I'll give you the full amount in cash within 21 days, and guarantee one-year employment for each of Conn's employees. How does that work for you?" I reeled with the offer, falling into a chair near the phone.

Two weeks later, George called again. He had done the evaluations, and the price he recited was exactly double what my grandfather had hoped for. Mr. Gardiner invited me to his office, located on the top floor of the Toronto-Dominion Tower. There, at 4pm, I was to meet his son Michael, with whom I went to school. Michael would have the certified cheque ready for me.

I pulled my best suit out of the closet, found a crisp white shirt still in the plastic from the dry cleaner and selected an appropriate tie. I had to look smart if I was to be picking up a sizeable cheque like the one awaiting me. As I began the drive downtown, a clap of thunder echoed nearby. A second later a torrential rainfall hit, pouring tons of water onto the streets of Toronto. I pulled the car into a parking lot underneath the TD Tower. Pushing the button for the uppermost floor, the elevator sped to the top. The doors parted and there Michael Gardiner greeted me. He lead me into a small meeting room, and handed me a certified cheque. Now all I had to do was sign over all the 65 certificates; one for each racehorse. One by one, I read each name silently to myself. Each brought its own memory, and the experience made me a little melancholy.

The sale represented an end to the Smythe racehorse legacy. I signed 64, but hesitated on the last one. Michael picked up on my reticence. "Tommy, I remember how you used to talk to me about "Jammed Lucky" and what he meant to you and your family," he began. "Keep that one for yourself. We'll move him to our stable. I've already talked this over with my Dad. We'll look after him, breed him and mail you half the fee from his stud service." I tried to thank Michael, but the words wouldn't come. "Jammed Lucky" was a 21-year-old stallion that we loved. He had sired "Jammed Lovely," Conn's Queen's Cup-winning filly from our Centennial celebration.

As my mind drifted, Michael broke the awkward silence. "Tommy, you'd better run. It's 10 to five and you have to get over to the Royal Bank Tower. They close at five." Down the express elevator I went, and ran for the front door. So much for my best suit I thought, as I took off in a sprint through the downpour. I got to the Royal Bank Tower just as the security guard turned the lock in the door. "Wait," I hollered, but he just shook his head. I pulled out the seven-figure cheque and slammed it up to the glass. I don't think the guard had ever seen that many zeroes in his life. He unlocked the door and ushered me in. The bank manager stepped out from his office and welcomed me. I placed the money in a high interest fund and by 5:30pm was on my way home.

Neither a light meal nor a quick shower relaxed me. My head was spinning, and I tried to doze, but sleep wouldn't come. Then, a huge crash of thunder married to a bright flash of lightning shook the entire house. I rolled over and glanced at the clock — 11:11. Tommy and Christy were frightened awake and ran to our bed. "Don't worry, kids," I comforted them. "Everything is just fine." And it was. With a hug, they crawled into bed with us. I closed my eyes. "Thank you Grandpa," I thought. After this communication from Conn and Stafford, sleep captured me and buried me in its comfort.

Years after Dad died, Dot asked me to divide all the cottage property that had been left to her into four lots, one each for Vicky, Mary, Elizabeth and me. My sister Vicky and I had been paying some of the cottage's taxes, insurance and incidentals for my mom. When I finished all the preparations, I went to the Registry Hall in Bracebridge. As I entered the office I decided to register my share of the property in my children's names, with me as commissioner to cover all expenses. I walked out of the office delighted with my decision, and kept the secret for 18 years.

At long last, I let the kids know that in actuality they owned the Muskoka property. Tommy and Christy were thrilled and made the mature decision to sell the property.

My wife Penny is a real estate agent and handled the sale. Soon after the property was listed, we received a cash offer, close to the asking price, no conditions attached and a 21-day closing. The purchaser was Steve Yzerman, captain of the Detroit Red Wings. I spoke with Steve personally and discussed the sale. I mentioned that the property had been in the Smythe family for many years and held the presence of 11 Stanley Cups. With Steve's recent win, that would make the total 12. Steve was excited. "You have a deal, Tommy." As Steve Yzerman uttered his confirmation, the second hand was sweeping around to the top of the clock. The time? 11:11.

My lawyer, Bob Durno, was working on the final paperwork to complete the sale. The day was getting late, and I wondered if something was wrong. Finally, the phone rang. It was Bob. "Tom, we have a problem," he started to explain. "The last piece of the original land is still in Stafford's name. I can't believe it. That bastard Ballard is still trying to screw you around even in death. He never looked after it as the executor of Stafford's will." It was 4:44. I felt reassured that Stafford was letting me know that everything would turn out fine.

Bob told me he'd convince Yzerman's American lawyer that there was no other Stafford Smythe, and that the deal could proceed. "Get some papers drawn up that correct the error, then once you and your Mom sign them, faxed them over." It was a stressful day, waiting to see if Harold would have his last laugh, but when the phone rang, it was a relieved lawyer who told me, "Congratulations Tom. Your children have sold their cottage to Yzerman." The clock on my desk read 11:11. Bob explained that he had to do some paperwork, and that his office would call me when it was time for me to drive over and pick up the cheque. The call came, and I made my way to the law office. After I signed the necessary papers, Bob Durno handed me the cheque. "Bob, turn your desk clock my way for a second," I asked. Yes, it was 4:44.

I phoned Tommy and Christy and told them the news. Our bank was closed on the Monday, so we met with our bank manager Tuesday at noon. Tommy signed the papers placed in front of him. And was on his way before the ink had a chance to dry, but not before he gave me a hug that nearly broke my back. Christy was more meticulous, asking that everything be explained so she understood everything clearly.

Once satisfied, she and I walked to the parking lot together. She said, "Dad, Tommy and I have something we want to give you." She opened the trunk and pulled out the sign that had hung in front of the cottage for so many years — "Uncle Tom's

Cabin." My emotions got the best of me. Christy gave me a hug that lasted forever. I sat in the car unable to move. When I regained my composure, I turned the key in the ignition. As the dashboard lit up, I took a look at the time. It was 4:44. I realized that I had just executed half of my will — and didn't even have to die to do it. There were times through the years when I questioned whether I'd been a good enough father to Tommy and Christy. Long work hours, ill health, a marriage to their mother that hadn't worked out. But now I knew for certain that I was.

When I told my priest, Monsignor Robitaille from St. Michael's Cathedral in Toronto about my extraordinary links and coincidences with the times "11:11" and "4:44," the edges of his mouth curled up into a huge smile. He felt that these occurrences were miracles and that I was an inordinately fortunate man.

Chapter Twenty-Four

The Conn Smythe Charitable Foundation

Before he passed away, my Grandfather asked me a question that would dramatically affect my adult life. He asked if I would continue the Conn Smythe Charitable Foundation. Way back in World War II, as Conn was lying on the battlefield with shrapnel pressed against his spine, he promised himself that, should he survive, he would use profits from the Gardens and his stable of racehorses to build a special foundation. Between 1947 and 1960, my grandfather paid off the loan to Percy Gardiner. Once he was clear of his debt, he founded the Conn Smythe Charitable Foundation. During the early days, he had lots of help from friends and associates, including Hap Day, my Dad, his brother Hugh and sister Miriam. The Conn Smythe Charitable Foundation was a source of immense pride to Conn. Thousands of Canadians have been helped through its generosity.

But as his health began to fail, my grandfather truly felt that the Foundation would die with him. His wife Irene was gone, and my Dad and Miriam were too. Uncle Hugh as a doctor wouldn't be able to devote all his time to the Foundation. So when Grandpa asked me if I'd be willing to give part of my life to help people, there was no decision to make. I proudly accepted his offer and let him know that I looked forward to working with the foundation members.

This Foundation had been set up to ensure that money was made available to help any number of different charities, in Toronto and across Canada. Grandpa had special affection for certain charitable organizations, and asked that they be included for as long as the Foundation was able to support them. Among them: the Ontario Society for Crippled Children (later renamed the Easter Seals Society) and Toronto's Variety Village, Covenant House, Second Harvest and the Bob Rumball Association for the Deaf.

The focus of the foundation has targeted three areas of concern: 1) to help send children with special needs to summer camp, 2) to assist in helping the homeless of all ages and 3) to help medical research in specialized areas. And because of my interest in Canadian aboriginal culture, the Foundation has endeavoured to give as much aid as possible to Native Canadian charities as well. My grandfather also insisted that administrative expenses be kept to an absolute minimum so that the overwhelming majority of the funds would go directly to where they were needed.

Twice a year, in June and November, the Foundation chooses 20 to 30 groups to donate money to. A list of the recipients in June 2000 offers an idea of the width and breadth of our support.

Big Brothers of Toronto, Bob Rumball Association for the Deaf-Camp, Camp Awakening, Children's Aid Foundation, Child Psychotherapy Foundation of Canada, Covenant House, Dorothy Ley Hospice, Downtown Care-Ring, Downtown Churchworkers Association-Moorelands Camp, Eva's Place, Friends of Oochigeas, Hopeworks-The Second Century of Yonge Street Mission, Huntington Society of Canada-Camp, Interval House, Jessie's Centre for Teenagers, Kid's Help Phone, Kidney Foundation of Canada-Camp, Rose Cherry House, Schizophrenia Society of Ontario, Scott Mission, Second Harvest, South Muskoka Hospital Foundation, Starlight Children's Foundation of Canada, Sully's Toronto Youth and Athletic Club, Trails Youth Initiatives, United Way of Greater Toronto, Variety Village, Wellspring, Windfall Clothing Service, Windreach Farm

Before his death in 1990, Hap Day was part of the Foundation. Hap had been joined at the hip with my grandfather for years. When Conn bought the Toronto St. Pats, he came with the team. Hap captained the Leafs for the entire time he played with them, between 1926 and 1937. He later coached the team, and led them to five Stanley Cups. As general manager, Hap stayed with Toronto until the Silver Seven came in to run the organization. Day was also a minority owner and general manager of C. Smythe for Sand for 30 years. He left the company when he left the Maple Leafs. At that time, Hap started his own business, manufacturing axe handles in St. Thomas, Ontario. In spite of being pushed out of the Maple Leaf organization, Conn and Hap remained great friends, and Day was a most willing participant in Grandpa's Foundation, even after Conn's death. Twice a year, he'd make the pilgrimage from St. Thomas to Toronto for the 10:30 morning meeting. He would actively participate in our discussions, then return back home. Hap Day was one of the classiest gentlemen you'd ever care to meet.

Doug Musgrave and I attended UCC together, and became best friends, a friendship which has spanned over 40 years. The Foundation doesn't take applications from charitable organizations for support. It's up to Doug and I to identify the best possible recipients in keeping with Conn's original plan. We review possible charities, meet with their executives and then table a report for the rest of the Foundation's members. It's rare that the members of the Foundation ever turn down a charity seeking support. Following receipt of the funds, we require the charity to submit a report detailing how the Foundation's grant is helping them.

George Mara came from a wealthy family, and neither his mother nor father had any intention of letting him play hockey for a living, although he was certainly capable of being in the

NHL. George had played with the Toronto Marlboros Junior team, with the Toronto Staffords senior team and with the Montreal Royals of the Quebec Senior Hockey League. As a member of the RCAF Flyers hockey team, George won an Olympic gold medal for Canada in 1948. His parents wanted him to follow in the family business, which imported wine and liquor into Canada. His draw to hockey was so strong, that in the late '40s, George snuck away and showed up at the Toronto Maple Leafs training camp. He had been invited for his hockey prowess and was performing very well. But then Conn stepped onto the players' bench and interrupted the practice to ask, "Who drives the Ford convertible parked out front?" It was George's. When Conn realized it was a prospects car, he shouted, "Forget it — let him go. He comes from money, and he'll never have the hunger to play professional hockey." George Mara successfully ran the family liquor business for decades, had a short stint as president of Maple Leaf Gardens in 1970, and is now an integral part of the Conn Smythe Charitable Foundation.

My Uncle Hugh is my Dad's younger brother, and third child born to Conn and Irene. Like Stafford and I, Hugh had also been the stickboy for the Leafs — his tenure was in the early 1940s. Uncle Hugh had been a fine young hockey player when, at the age of 18, he contracted tuberculosis. For two years, he lay in a darkened bedroom, unable to move. During that time, Hugh decided he was going to dedicate his life to medicine. My dad was angry when Hugh decided to take up medicine, as Stafford felt he could have done very well in hockey. For a number of years, Hugh combined his two passions as one of the Maple Leafs team doctors.

Every Sunday morning between 10 and noon, the ice at Maple Leaf Gardens was made available to executives, staff, players and their families to enjoy a scrimmage. When I was 10 or 11, Uncle Hugh and I were playing on opposing teams, and he continually stick handled past me. Over and over he'd make a great move that left me spinning. Finally, I got frustrated, and the next time he came down the ice, I checked him as hard as I could. It would have made Don Cherry proud, but not my uncle. He was ready to drop his gloves and go toe-to-toe with me. The gate to the players' bench was unlatched, and I just happened to catch Hugh in such a way that he hit the open door and caught his knee, in the process doing some serious damage. The fact that he still brings it up more than 40 years later means that he may have forgiven me, but he sure hasn't forgotten.

After my Dad died, Uncle Hugh was extremely supportive. He offered to take a couple of years away from his practice in order to help take control of Maple Leaf Gardens away from Harold Ballard. We made a valiant attempt to acquire the Gardens, but sadly it just wasn't meant to be.

Dr. Hugh Smythe is an indispensable part of the Conn Smythe Charitable Foundation and has orchestrated the move of millions of dollars to underprivileged charities.

Chapter Twenty-Five

A Hull of a Shot

Throughout my life I was a permanent fixture at the Gardens and had the privileged opportunity to meet and befriend many of the most famous NHL names that entered the building. In my teens, I remember a time the Blackhawks arrived in Toronto. It was during the 1960-61 season — the last year Chicago won the Stanley Cup. At the core of the team were sharpshooters Bobby Hull and Stan Mikita, both of whom went on to earn hockey's greatest recognition, an induction in the Hockey Hall of Fame.

I arrived at the Gardens early to watch Chicago practise for their game that night against the Leafs. It was a thrill to be there and have a chance to meet the team. One by one, the players skated off to the dressing room: Glenn Hall, Moose Vasko, Kenny Wharram and the rest. But Hull and Mikita stayed on the ice working on their shots. Mikita took a powerful slapshot that pounded against the end boards but cracked the blade of his stick in the process. His next shot saw the puck take an unusual course, dipping and curving before it bulged the netting in the corner of the goal. Mikita looked at Hull and grinned. The two had discovered the benefit of a curved stick blade. Up until that era, hockey sticks had virtually flat blades.

I sat in the stands and watched as both players retreated to their dressing room. Within a few minutes, Hull and Mikita returned. Apparently they had located a plumber's blowtorch and used its heat to further warp the wood blades of their sticks. They lined up a dozen pucks each and began shooting. Slapshots flew everywhere — rifle shots into the net, booming shots against the boards and stray shots landing in the seats. After the dozen shots, they moved out to centre ice and looked towards the stands in the southeast corner of the Gardens. A quick glance and I saw what they saw: Harold Ballard's private box seats, carved into the brickwork just behind the net at glass level. Bob and Stan shook hands, then skated off the ice. As they stepped through the gate on their way to the dressing room, Hull saw me standing there and called out. "Hey Tommy, make sure you're here to watch the pre-game warm up. Mikita and I have a $5,000 bet going to see who can hit Ballard in his box from centre ice."

Not wanting to miss such an event, I took my seat early and watched as Ballard entered his box and the Blackhawks stepped onto the ice. Mikita and Hull loosened up, then took a couple of shots that rattled the end glass. Harold never flinched as he continued reading his program. Each player fired a couple more shots, but neither cleared the glass. Until, with a broad smile, Hull wound up again, and struck the puck with incredible force. All I saw was a streak of black clear the glass, then take a dip and enter Ballard's box. CRACK! The puck caught Ballard right between the eyes, driving him out of his chair, backward into his box and out of my view. At centre ice, Hull and Mikita were in tears of laughter.

Ballard survived with only a few stitches and a broken pair of glasses and Hull walked away $5,000 richer.

Chapter Twenty-Six

Cottage Life

"Tom, do you know who Colleen and Gordie Howe are?" my wife Penny asked one day. I laughed, "You're kidding, right?" "No," she said, "I have no idea. A lady called here before you got home. She said she was Colleen Howe, and that she and Gordie were coming into town this weekend. They wanted to have dinner with us." I wondered how could a University graduate who has lived in Toronto her entire life know absolutely nothing about hockey. Friends have teased Penny about the "Howe story" for years.

Having grown up so involved in hockey, it's somewhat refreshing to be married to someone so oblivious to that world. It keeps me grounded, makes me realize that there is a big world out there that doesn't revolve around a stick and a puck.

Around the time of my first operations, my marriage to Anne started to unravel and we separated. I lived alone for a year, struggling to get along. My life had changed drastically — I was no longer able to eat normally, and medication and nutrition became huge parts of my life. Friends and acquaintances visited me often, and this helped me get through some difficult times. One of my regular visitors was my office partner, Penny Brown.

Penny really took an interest in making sure I received proper nutrition. With each visit, we got closer. Soon, she was visiting each morning on her way to work. We quickly realized that we had a number of common interests, although hockey isn't one of them. After awhile, I looked at Penny, and realized she was a beautiful woman, inside and out. I hadn't looked at her in that way before.

In 1992, we were married and I insist that Penny not only changed my life, but likely saved it as well. She is meticulous in ensuring that I get proper treatment. And was instrumental in weaning me off the enormous amount of morphine I was taking to dull the pain.

A part of my life away from hockey is our cottage life, although I still get a taste of hockey when I'm there. My pal Bill Harris, the Marlboro star who was drafted in the first round by the Islanders, was one of the first cottage purchasers of his hockey generation. Today, it's not unusual to be in Muskoka and see Eric and Brett Lindros, Shane Corson or Paul Coffey out on the lake boating, likely in a Scarab, or Donzi, or be in Georgian Bay's Wasaga Beach area and see the tremendous fan support of their local beloved hero Jason Arnott.

From the time I was born, our family had visited Conn and Irene's cottage on Lake Simcoe. Dad and Mom later bought a cottage, on Lake Joseph in Muskoka. We spent our summers there beginning in 1962, the summer of my sixteenth birthday.

That same summer, I met a guy named John Blair who worked at the Port Sandfield Marina. He and I became good friends, and he helped me get a job there. The owner, Alf Mortimer, became friends with Dad, and introduced him to his employees and customers from all over Muskoka. Ironically, many of Alf's customers and visitors happened to be Leafs — guys like Dick Duff, Frank Mahovlich and Eddie Shack. The hockey community is close-knit, and we would often run into Maple Leaf players during our summers in Muskoka. Later, this circle would extend to include other players from all over the league.

John Blair and Alf Mortimer had a passion for antique wooden boats and proceeded to teach me all they new. A sizeable number of these boats still cruise the lakes in the Muskoka region. I absorbed every amount of information I could and when John would travel the waters to service boats, both antique and modern, I would go with him to watch and learn.

The Muskoka region, known as Ontario's playground for the rich and famous has been the perfect getaway for families for close to 100 years. When World War I broke out, Canada's Prime Minister Sir Robert Borden was summoned from his Muskoka vacation. Woodrow Wilson, a U.S. President, vacationed in the Muskokas, as did Orville Wright, Mr. "First in Flight." Various branches of the Eaton family have had cottages in the Muskokas for close to a century. I enjoyed the Muskoka area for almost 30 years, but returned to my grandparents' favoured cottage area in 1990 when I moved back to Lake Simcoe for my summer weekends.

Conn was angry with Dad for having left Lake Simcoe for the Muskokas in 1962. It was all Stafford, Dot and I could do to convince Conn to visit. My grandfather complained about the length of the drive, but did eventually join us and in spite of his objections, had a great time. Dad brought him over to the Port Sandfield Marina where I held a summer job pumping gas and cleaning boats. Alf Mortimer, the marina's owner, took a great picture of the three generations of Smythe men, a shot that still hangs in the marina as well as in my home.

As a 12-year-old boy, I attended Camp Ahmek, in Algonquin Park. It was a long train ride from Lake Simcoe to Canoe Lake. The train depot where we disembarked was about a mile from the camp, and it took a long, hot, sweaty walk to get there. Once there, I walked into the main dining room to meet my counselor, who happened to be Brian Conacher. Brian later went on to play with the Marlboros, and graduated to play a handful of games with the Leafs in 1961-62 and 1965-66. He joined the big club formally for two full seasons — the Stanley-Cup-winning 1966-67 season, the following year.

While at camp I met Dr. Taylor Statten, a man I came to know and respect tremendously through the years. "Tom, come lend us a hand carving this totem pole and I'll tell you some stories about the Indians who first lived on this ground centuries ago." For two hours, I was transfixed by the legends of Canada's aboriginal people. Each day, I would return to learn more. I returned to camp for the next few summers and eventually became a counselor for two seasons until my commitment to hockey took over my summers. But the teachings of Dr. Taylor Statten have stayed with me since, and to this day, I ensure that our aboriginal partners are well addressed by the Conn Smythe Charitable Foundation.

My last year at camp, I found an old wooden boat destined for destruction. It was lying out in a baseball field, and hadn't seen a drop of lake water in well over a decade. The wood was entirely sun-drenched and had lost its lustre, and had been stripped years earlier of any of its chrome ornaments. I rescued it from being burnt by offering to buy it, with my mind set on giving it to Dad as a Father's Day gift. My thousand-dollar offer was snapped up, and I became the proud owner of a decrepit, leaking shell of a once beautiful boat.

Before presenting it to my father, I patched it up the best I could, and set sail. My trip from Gravenhurst, which should have taken about an hour, ended up taking six. There were leaks everywhere, and I couldn't bail the water fast enough. Finally, I gave up in Port Carling, where I asked Dad to meet me. He loved it. The boat turned out to be an antique Minett, a brand of boat indigenous to the Muskoka region. It had been built around 1925 or '26. Further research revealed that it had once belonged to the Eaton family, and had been named "Marmilwood" after their cottage.

My father began a new hobby — restoring antique boats. In fact, his activity launched a whole new revolution in boat restoration in the area. People from all over Muskoka were interested in seeing the progress of his boat. The man doing most of the work was Ron Butson, an experienced boatman with a tremendous amount of experience in bringing old boats back to life. Three area men who had actually been involved in the boat's original 1925-26 construction, pulled their creaking rocking chairs up near the stern to offer Ron their advice.

My thousand-dollar investment took three or four years and about $12,000 to restore. But after many years of enjoyment, the boat was sold for over $125,000.

Because it had originally been named "Marmilwood," and to pay homage to Maple Leaf star Frank Mahovlich, we named the boat, "The Big M." The name was written in crayon on the stern, and when the stern was replaced, there was "The Big M," gleaming in chrome. Frank Mahovlich came to our cottage to christen the boat once it was lake-ready, breaking a bottle of champagne against its polished bow.

The day after, Dad drove the lakes, visiting as many of his friends as possible. After several hours, he returned, and called out to me from "The Big M" which was about 100 feet from the dock, "Please land this for me, Tommy. I've had too many congratulatory drinks." Dad jumped overboard and swam to the ladder at the dock. I became "The Big M's" chauffeur after that.

Years later, Dad introduced my son to boating. It was July 20, 1970, and there was nine-day-old Tommy Junior propped up in a dough box sitting on Dad's lap. Tommy was the only grandchild my father ever lived to meet, and to know that the Smythe name would be continued for another generation made my Dad proud.

"The Big M" carried on for years. It won so many restoration awards at antique boat shows that, after a while, we were no longer eligible to compete. Each year, several Toronto Maple

Leaf players would drive up for the Muskoka antique boat show, then stop in to say hello to us and see that amazing Maple Leaf blue-and-white Canadian flag which flew over our cottage.

Chapter Twenty-Seven

Honoured Member

Inside the beautiful heritage building at the corner of Yonge and Front Streets in the heart of Toronto's downtown, are housed the names and faces of hockey players, officials and builders who have been selected as Honoured Members of the Hockey Hall of Fame. There is one name missing: Stafford Smythe.

My father did so much to help build the game of hockey. By devising a farm system that began with boys just reaching their teens, the Toronto Maple Leafs were assured a steady stream of excellent hockey players. If the boys were good enough, they'd accelerate through the ranks from peewee to bantam to midget to Junior B to Junior A to — the ultimate goal — a shot with the Toronto Maple Leafs. Simultaneously, Stafford and his team were securing players from across the country to be fed into the system for the Leafs. Hall of Fame members who moved through the system under Stafford's guidance include George Armstrong, Gerry Cheevers (who began his career with the Leafs but was lost in the draft to the Bruins), Tim Horton, David Keon, Frank Mahovlich, Brad Park (who went through the Leafs system but entered the NHL with the New York Rangers) and Bob Pulford. And then there are the stars who haven't made the Hockey Hall of Fame, but who played excellent NHL hockey. They include

Lou Angotti, Bob Baun, Carl Brewer, Arnie Brown, Wayne Carleton, Dave Dryden, Dick Duff, Ron Ellis, Billy Harris, Jim McKenny, Al McNeil, Mike Murphy, Bob Nevin, Rod Seiling, Brit Selby, Gary Smith, Peter Stemkowski, Ron Stewart, Dale Tallon, Steve Vickers and Mike Walton.

The Leafs junior system has also spawned an unusually high number of players who went on to coach or manage in the NHL. These ranks include Lou Angotti, George Armstrong, Charlie Burns, Gerry Cheevers, John McLellan, Al McNeil, Gerry Meehan, Mike Murphy, Harry Neale, Mike Nykoluk, Brad Park, Bob Pulford and Ron Stewart.

Stafford Smythe was president of the Toronto Maple Leafs for four Stanley Cup victories, emblematic of National Hockey League supremacy. He was also the managing director of the four Toronto Marlboro teams who won the Memorial Cup for junior hockey supremacy. The most valuable player in the Memorial Cup series is awarded the Stafford Smythe Memorial Trophy.

The list of Dad's peers who have been selected as honoured members in the Builders category includes my grandfather Conn, Harold Ballard and Punch Imlach. Conn's contributions stand entirely on their own. As founder of the Toronto Maple Leafs, builder of Maple Leaf Gardens and a visionary he, with the assistance of the five other owners of Original Six hockey teams, helped develop the game of hockey we know today. As for Harold and Punch, both are worthy Hockey Hall of Fame members, however neither contributed anything that my father did not.

Some naysayers will be prompted to refer to my father's fraud and theft charges as reason alone to be kept out of the Hockey Hall of Fame. But these charges did not hinder Ballard's induction.

Other than the health of my family, there is nothing more in the world I wish for than for my father to be selected an Honoured Member in the Builders category of the Hockey Hall of Fame. When that day finally arrives, as a tribute to him, I will have the faded engravings on his Stanley Cup ring repaired and on the day of the induction, I will donate some of my many pieces of Toronto Maple Leaf hockey historical memorabilia to the Hockey Hall of Fame.

Chapter Twenty-Eight

Bricks and Mortar

A building is nothing more than the sum of it parts. In reality, Maple Leaf Gardens is just a colossal pile of bricks and mortar. Nothing more, nothing less. But what gives a building its value is the personality that has been developed within its walls. Maple Leaf Gardens has now been sold, and its fate lies in the hands of a developer. It will remain an arena, but in a scaled-down version more appropriate for junior hockey or Leaf practices. It will never be the same. It can never be the same.

It takes stories to give a building personality. Some of these stories grow larger in stature with the passage of time, and they eventually become legends.

Maple Leaf Gardens will always be known as the edifice that introduced the National Hockey League to the Kid Line, in the 1930s. The Herculean stories of Charlie Conacher, Busher Jackson and Joe Primeau terrorizing opposing teams on the Gardens ice are paralleled to the equally Bunyan-esque stories of the trio off the ice. Gentleman Joe Primeau seemed to carry his persona from his Leaf uniform to his civilian clothes, while Conacher and Jackson lived hard and fast, and both men met their demise early. My grandfather specifically singled out Jackson for exclusion from the Hockey Hall of Fame, citing his alcoholism as conduct unbecoming an honoured member. It took many years, but all three Maple Leaf line mates are now revered members of the Hockey Hall of Fame.

Among other things, Maple Leaf Gardens will be remembered for being the home of Irvine Ace Bailey. A former St. Pats star, Bailey became a Leaf when my grandfather bought the team.

His uniform's number six is one of only two numbers the Leafs have retired, never to be worn again. The source of his legacy took place in Boston, when Bailey was crushed to the ice by Eddie Shore, a Bruins star defenseman. It was December 12, 1933. Ace lay on the ice close to death, his skull fractured. While Leaf trainers and medical staff attended to him, his Leaf teammates fought the Boston Bruins in his defense. Ace Bailey recovered, but not after having been administered the last rites. He was never to play hockey again. Bailey is also in the Hockey Hall of Fame.

Maple Leaf Gardens introduced hockey fans to Syl Apps and Ted Kennedy. The two are generally regarded as the finest on-ice leaders the Toronto Maple Leafs ever presented. Apps was the smooth-skating, gentlemanly former Olympic athlete who served as the Leafs captain through parts of the 1940s, and later moved into the political arena. Kennedy replaced Apps as captain in 1948, and was equally adept at firing up his troops. His skating was anything but smooth; his demeanor anything but gentlemanly. Yet the pair collectively led the Leafs to seven Stanley Cups during one of its most fertile periods. Both Apps and Kennedy have been included in the Hockey Hall of Fame.

Maple Leaf Gardens will forever live through the retired number five that hung from the rafters of the Gardens and now hangs from the ceiling of the Air Canada Centre. Bill Barilko had only scratched the surface of what might have been an all-star career when his plane crashed in northern Ontario following a fishing trip during the summer of 1951. To add to the drama, Barilko had scored the winning goal in overtime to give the Toronto Maple Leafs the Stanley Cup just four months earlier. It was the fourth Stanley Cup of Barilko's abbreviated five-year career.

Maple Leaf Gardens will always be remembered for its four Stanley Cups in the 1960s. Spearheaded by Punch Imlach, the team boasts an inordinately high number of Hall of Fame members. In its esteemed ranks are captain George Armstrong; Andy Bathgate; goaltender extraordinaire Johnny Bower; iron man Tim Horton; Red Kelly; mercury-skated Dave Keon, the Big M Frank Mahovlich; Bert Olmstead; Marcel Pronovost; Bob Pulford; Terry Sawchuk and Allan Stanley.

Maple Leaf Gardens will be remembered for its dark side, too. At the conclusion of the 1970s, a team that mounted a considerable attack with Darryl Sittler, Lanny McDonald, Errol Thompson, Dave Tiger Williams, Ian Turnbull and Borje Salming was methodically dismantled piece by piece under the control of Harold Ballard. The team suffered through the humiliation, yet the diehard Toronto hockey fans maintained their support and the Gardens continued to sell-out. Ballard's popularity plummeted and Toronto fans felt that under his control, the Leafs would never reclaim the glory of the Stanley Cup winning Smythe years. He traded away talented players and prospects to such a degree that the Toronto hockey community questioned his motives. 1979 saw Leaf superstar Lanny McDonald traded to the Colorado Rockies, in a move, which devastated the team emotionally and physically. Player's moods were at an all time low. Many were angered by Ballard's decision and trashed the Leaf dressing room. During the early 80's, Ballard traded away and released much of the Leafs best talent and by doing so finished the decade with a devastating record, finishing in last place in their division two seasons and dead last in the league through six seasons.

Maple Leaf Gardens rose to glory once again in the early 1990s. Sparked by the moxy of Doug Gilmour, the sheer power of Wendel Clark and the sterling goaltending of Felix Potvin, the 1992-93 team came one game away from Toronto's first Stanley Cup final since 1967. Gilmour's wrap-around goal in overtime against St. Louis will be forever etched in Leaf fans' memories. And Wendel's pummeling of Los Angeles tough guy Marty McSorley to avenge a hit on Gilmour stirred the Gardens spirit. In the end, it was the Great One, Wayne Gretzky who shut the door on the Leafs Stanley Cup dreams that season. His hat trick in game seven moved the Los Angeles Kings on to the finals versus Montreal.

Wayne Gretzky was one of the few players in the NHL who could enter any team's home rink and receive an ovation. His style, ability and character afforded him a genial welcome by all fans of the game, even when his name would appear multiple times on the score sheet and his team walk away victorious. As much as all of Toronto hoped for a birth in the Stanley Cup finals that year, the Leaf's devastating loss to LA was lightened by the thrill of watching the Great One play his game and earn another chance at the trophy he so much deserved.

It's just bricks and mortar, and a whole lot of fantastic memories. My grandfather's blood and sweat permeate through the old building. It's a storied franchise, to be sure. My father's thumbprint stayed on the team for 25 years. With Darryl Sittler's trade to Philadelphia in January 1982, the last of my father's players or draft picks played with the Leafs.

Players talk about the immense pride they feel pulling on the Toronto Maple Leaf sweater. There were few as proud as Dave Tiger Williams.

Tiger was drafted by Toronto from the Swift Current Broncos in the 1974 Amateur Draft. The first day he arrived in Toronto, he walked into Maple Leaf Gardens and came into Doug Laurie Sports to introduce himself to me. He conveyed his sentiment regarding my father's recent death and acknowledged that he was aware that my Dad was the one who had seen him play years before and endorsed his pick in the draft. He expressed his thrill of becoming a Maple Leaf and how it had been a dream to play for the team since lacing up his skates as a child. He told me his concern regarding his skating abilities and asked who he'd have to knock out to be chosen to play. Tiger was a humorous guy. His candid mannerism always left me in tears of laughter. I told him that if he let me watch him practise a few times, I might be able to suggest some ways to help.

I watched Tiger every day. Each morning when he arrived at the Gardens, he'd drop in to see me and ask how he was doing. I'd give him the same answer: "Fine, Tiger. You're doing fine. Just keep working at it." After watching him for several days at training camp, I finally felt I had some ideas that would help his skating. One morning, he came by my office as usual, and it was this time that I greeted him with a challenge. "Hey Tiger, meet me here at the end of your practise. I've got some ideas I want to bounce off you."

After his shower, Tiger came by my office. I began, by telling what would improve his skating. "From the player's bench, run up the stairs to the top seats as fast as you can, touch the wall and run back down to the bench. Do that a couple of times each day, then build up to three or four times over the course of a couple of weeks. When you get back to the bench from your run, lace up your skates again. Go to one of the face-off circles by the net. Lean in and skate as fast as you can around that circle 10 times. Go to the other face-off circle and skate it 10 times, but in the opposite direction." Tiger rolled his eyes at me, "Tommy, whaddya trying to do to me?" "Wait" I continued. "There's more." I had worked with players my entire life and knew how to get the most from their abilities so I had Tiger work on his skating every day. I promised him that his efforts would pay off.

Each morning after practice, Tiger diligently went through my skating drills and after two weeks, Tiger came in to the store again. "Okay Tommy, after the team practice today, I want you to lock up the store and come watch my workout." Tiger said. I went in and watched the end of the Leafs practice. Out came Tiger. He glanced my way and flew up the stairs to the greys, and proceeded to make the trip 10 times. My legs hurt just watching him. After the tenth circuit, he pulled on his skates and took to the ice for his face-off circle exercises. I couldn't believe that the man skating was the player I had seen just a few weeks before. Jim Gregory, the general manager, wandered over to say hi, and remarked on how Tiger's skating had improved.

The next day, Jim Gregory came in to my office and handed me an order form for customized sticks for Tiger Williams. "Tom, don't tell him, okay?" Jim asked. "Let him stew a little longer."

It was difficult to keep this secret. With every day, there'd be another query from Tiger. "Heard anything yet?" I lied through my teeth, "Nope. Not a word, Tiger." After a few days, Tiger's sticks arrived. I phoned Gregory to let him know. He tried to compliment me. "Tommy, your Dad would have been proud of the way you worked with Tiger and enhanced his game." I thanked Jim for his compliment and how both he and my father were equally responsible for Tiger's improvement, as it was both he and my father who taught me everything I knew about hockey. Jim wasn't one to acknowledge compliments well and ignored my remarks. Instead he asked me to tell Tiger the good news, that he had been given a position on the Leafs roster.

Just like every day before, Tiger came into the store and asked if I'd heard anything. This time was different. "Tiger, follow me downstairs," I said. Unaware of the reasoning, Tiger followed me to the basement, where leaned up against the wall in a rack was a supply of sticks. I handed him one with "#22" and "Williams" printed down the shaft. "Tommy. I've made it," he screamed, and burst into tears. He sat there for 20 minutes, starring at his sticks with tears in his eyes occasionally mumbling phrases like "I can't believe it," "This is the dream of my life" and "Thank you." "Congratulations," I interrupted. "Now get out there to practise. Gregory's waiting for you."

I watched Dave Tiger Williams establish himself in the NHL through the seventies. For a guy who would run up 300 penalty minutes in a season, he was a fine goal scorer, consistently scoring about 20 goals each season he was in Toronto. And statistics don't measure the entertainment value he brought to Toronto. Even though it's been more than 20 years since he pulled on a Leaf sweater for an NHL game, he still endures as one of the city's most popular athletes.

Tiger continued to visit me at Doug Laurie Sports on a regular basis. He always thanked my family and me for what we had done for him. I took him up to meet my grandfather one day, and Tiger was thrilled. "Wow. What an office," he exclaimed. After shaking Conn's hand, he continued to look at the three walls showcasing the Leaf captains holding the Stanley Cup through the years.

When training camp resumed the next September, Tiger dropped by and excitedly relayed that he'd gone to visit my grandfather's farm and spent time with one of his favourite hockey legends, Conn Smythe.

During the 1979-80 season, Punch Imlach traded Tiger to Vancouver.

My grandfather died in 1983. It made headlines in newspapers across Canada. My friend Rick Porter once again took care of a Smythe funeral, and Uncle Hugh was overseeing the arrangements with my help. The funeral took place in the same Muskoka church that we used to say goodbye to my Dad. I arrived early, and was feeling pretty low. I saw the hearse approaching with Conn's body, when someone behind me whispered, "My heart is broken just like yours." I whipped around and saw Tiger Williams. "Tiger." Thank you for coming. But what are you doing here? Aren't you supposed to be playing tonight in Vancouver?" I asked.

"Yeah Tom," he shrugged "I'm supposed to be, but I'm AWOL. The Canucks have fined me $10,000, but I really don't care. Today, I'm here for the Smythe family. I'm here for Conn, I'm here for your Dad and I'm here for you, Tommy. And I'm here for the day I found out I was going to be playing for the Toronto Maple Leafs when you first showed me my sticks.

Chapter Twenty-Nine

Farewell

The 1998-99 season was to be the last for the Toronto Maple Leafs at Maple Leaf Gardens. It was the end of an era for all hockey fans, but was probably a little more melancholy for me than most. We all have our memories, but the Smythe family has been so intrinsically tied to both the history of the Toronto Maple Leafs and to Maple Leaf Gardens that I couldn't help but feel a deep sense of personal loss.

The Toronto Maple Leafs owner, Steve Stavro, honoured me on behalf of the Smythe family by inviting me to drop the puck at the first game of this final season. I was joined by three others who had lineage in Toronto hockey history: Jim Thomson-Boulton, whose grandfather's company built the Gardens in 1931, Brian Young, whose grandfather was the Toronto Maple Leafs first season ticket-holder and Bernie Fournier, who joined the Gardens staff in 1952 and was representing the Gardens' employees. Leafs' captain Mats Sundin lined up opposite the captain of the Detroit Red Wings, Steve Yzerman, to take the ceremonial draw. I was thrilled to be there at centre ice — a place where I had enjoyed some of my greatest hockey moments. My thoughts rushed back to the Stanley Cup celebrations of 1962-63, 1963-64 and 1966-67, all of which took place right on that very spot, at centre ice of Maple Leaf Gardens.

The Toronto Maple Leafs had been playing solid hockey out of the Mutual Street Arena, located just south of Maple Leaf Gardens. But it was old and small, and only held 8,000 fans. My grandfather knew that in order to take advantage of the team's popularity, as well as to make any sort of profit, he needed the team to be housed in a larger location. No small amount of credit must go to Foster Hewitt, the legendary play-by-play announcer for the Leafs. ("Hello Canada and hockey fans in the United States and Newfoundland.") As much as the team had Conn's fingerprints all over it in regards to player personnel, Foster's impact was immense in a public relations sense. In an era long before television, computers and other diversions, families across Canada and the United States used radio as their primary source of entertainment. And when Foster called a Leaf game, families sat together, glued to the play-by-play coming from their radio set. The Toronto Maple Leafs quickly became Canada's team.

When my grandfather decided to build a new arena, he looked at a number of different locations. One was at the Lake Ontario waterfront near Yonge Street and what is now Lakeshore Boulevard, on property that was owned by the Toronto Harbour Commission. But this idea didn't pan out. There was a discussion of tearing down Knox College on Spadina near College, but the local residents opposed the demolition, so that spot was nixed as well. Finally, Eaton's was approached about some property it owned. The company offered a location a block north of Wood Street near Yonge, but my grandfather held out for some property at Carlton and Church, which he felt was more appropriate for the streetcar lines that passed would offer easier access for fans. Eaton's balked, worried that hockey fans weren't necessarily the kind of customers they were encouraging to shop at their new College Park location. But Conn was eventually able to convince Eaton's that the steady stream of potential customers attending Leaf games could only be a benefit to the new, modern Eaton's location nearby. Eaton's sold the property at Church and Carlton to Grandpa for $350,000. Now all that was needed was money to build the arena.

The actual site where Maple Leaf Gardens stands had historical significance long before Conacher, Kennedy, Keon or Clark ever touched a puck in the building. A battle during the Rebellion of 1837 took place where Carlton meets Church today. Toronto's first mayor, the 'rabid reformer,' William Lyon Mackenzie, led his followers into a skirmish on that site, and Sheriff Jarvis stopped Mackenzie and his troops in their tracks. This political melee led to the Battle of Montgomery's Tavern, where Mackenzie was defeated once again and was forced to leave the city in exile.

My grandfather and his executive team were natural salespeople. Even though cash flow was a problem across the spectrum of industries, they still were able to convince the Sun Life Insurance Company, the Bank of Commerce and Eaton's to bankroll most of what was needed to proceed with the construction.

Thomson Brothers Construction Company won the contract to build the Gardens, using the vision of Ross and MacDonald, an architectural firm from Montreal, which had designed Toronto landmarks such as the Royal York Hotel and Union Station. When Conn's own depleting cash flow threatened the completion of Maple Leaf Gardens, Frank Selke used his connections from his days as an electrician to implore the unions to allow their members to receive 20 percent of their wages in shares of Maple Leaf Gardens. Because work was so hard to come by at the time, practically any offer that included some cash was palatable to the workers. Many workers turned around and immediately sold their shares back to their unions or to Gardens officials because of the dire need for actual money in their pockets. It is unlikely that many held on to the stocks for any great length of time, but those that did would be extremely wealthy today. Shares in the Gardens continued to rise in value and often split, resulting in more stock and more money for the fortunate holders.

Just before Maple Leaf Gardens was built, the area around the corner of Carlton and Church Streets was comprised of a number of small houses and shops. A man named Alfred Ockley lived at 60 Carlton Street, an address that just a year later would be famous across North America. Beside Mr. Ockley, at 62 Carlton, was a Chinese laundry. At 64 was Mac the Mover. Keeling's Shoe Repair was at 66. Along Church Street, George Saspuntjis' confectionery was right on the corner of Carlton at 438 Church. The remainder of the block between Carlton and Wood Streets contained Little Wonder Beauty Parlour and a number of houses. In April 1931, these small houses and shops were demolished, and just over a month later, construction began.

Thirteen hundred men worked through the summer and autumn. After slightly less than six months, the puck was ready to be dropped for the first event at Maple Leaf Gardens. It was, appropriately enough, a hockey game. Six months was incredible, even to Conn. Whenever the building of the Gardens was discussed, Grandpa always shook his head and told us he had no idea and little faith that the job could be done so quickly, but also so well. Conn said, "It's a damned miracle that the thing got built at all. With lots of luck, hard work and plenty of prayers, the Gardens got built."

At 8:30 on the evening of November 12, 1931, after the 48th Highlanders and the Grenadier Guards had played "The Maple Leaf Forever" and "Happy Days Are Here Again," the Toronto Maple Leafs faced off against the Chicago Blackhawks. The first game ended in a 2-1 victory for the Blackhawks in front of a capacity crowd of 13, 233.

As was only appropriate, the final Toronto Maple Leaf game at Maple Leaf Gardens was against the Chicago Blackhawks, the same team, which had christened the arena with the Leafs 67 years and three months earlier. It was February 13, 1999, and the date had been marked on the schedule of all Leaf fans for close to a year. Nothing would stop me from attending the final game. Maple Leaf's owner, Steve Stavro had asked my wife Penny and I to be his guests. We had two seats behind Curtis Joseph in the Leafs goal. It was essential that a Smythe be in attendance at this game to atone for that Leaf loss on opening night in 1931.

As the players warmed up before the game, the excitement level increased. This was magic, pure and simple. Penny broke my anxiety. If you are not used to sitting behind the net, it seems like each shot is a potential missile into the crowd. So with each shot, Penny recoiled in fear. My wife isn't a huge hockey fan at the best of times, and this wasn't aiding her enjoyment of the game one bit.

For the ceremonial face-off, the Hawks made an exception and sent their assistant captain, former Leaf captain Doug Gilmour, to take the spot of captain Chris Chelios. Mats Sundin was his adversary across the face off circle. The man who scored the first goal in Maple Leaf Gardens, former Hawk Harold Mush March, partnered with Reginald Red Horner, Leaf Hall of Famer, to drop the ceremonial first puck. March and Horner had both participated in the first game at Maple Leaf Gardens, and they were given a standing ovation as they returned to help close it.

It was a decent game, but the Leafs were out of contention fairly early. After the first period, it was 2-0 Chicago. After the second, the Leafs had closed the gap, but were still behind 3-2. When Paul Morris announced, "Last minute to play in this period," the crowd stood and never took their seats again until the final buzzer had gone. The entire ice surface was awash in camera flashes capturing a moment in history. The third period had been all Blackhawks though, with Chicago potting three more goals. Bob Probert scored the final goal at Maple Leaf Gardens.

As the game came to a close, every one of the 15,726 in attendance, already on their feet, counted down the final seconds and broke into respectful, nostalgic applause in spite of the 6-2 loss for Toronto. The building shook from its convex roof to its blade-streaked floors by the concession stands. Spontaneous embraces broke out among the fans.

After 2,300 Maple Leaf home games and 19 Stanley Cups finals, the grand old building, Maple Leaf Gardens saw its last NHL contest. Tears mixed with laughter. My thoughts were of my grandfather Conn and my father Stafford. How I wish I could have shared this moment with them.

Epilogue

'Living the Moment'

I spent the initial 20 years of my life living at 44 Edgehill Road in Etobicoke, a prestigious street in an established suburb on the western edge of Toronto. During the 1950s, Ken and Joyce Seager purchased the home next door. Like my father's, Ken's employment required constant travel. During those absences, my mother and Mrs. Seager established a close friendship. The Seagers were a few years younger than my parents and just beginning to start a family at the time. While Ken was out of town, I remember that my mother assisted Joyce with her pregnancies and acted as midwife during her at-home deliveries.

My sister and I were never permitted in the house during the birth of Joyce's children. Instead, we were told to play outside and remain quiet. At the age of 10, this elaborate secrecy inspired my young curiosity to the point that, following the birth of Joyce's second child, I asked if I could see and hold her next baby when he or she was born. Joyce replied, "Tommy, of course you may." The next year, Joyce gave birth to a little girl. Remembering my request, Joyce invited me into the room. I sat in the rocking chair by the window and my mother gently placed the bathed newborn in my outstretched arms. I watched her intently and held her as vigilantly as I knew how. My eyes never left Nancy's little face, and a lifelong bond and friendship resulted.

Nancy now lives in Port Credit, Ontario. Several years ago, her friend, Lance Secretan wrote a book. He gave Nancy a copy and she passed it on to me. It was during a particularly painful time in my life and I was fighting to stay alive.

Inside the front cover was written a note: "Lance also has a deep passion for native culture ... thus this book. Hope you'll enjoy it. The title has probably been one of your personal credos throughout the last several years, Enjoy! Love, Nancy."

The book was entitled "Living the Moment — a sacred journey." It recounts the first story of Native Canadian Sacrament. It was the same story with which Dr. Taylor Statten held me spellbound at Camp Ahmek when I was 12. Circles always return. Live the moment and move on, but always stop to help someone in need. Givers will always receive; takers will not. These strong native sacraments have been my personal principals for life since I first heard them. They have helped me through all the fortune and misfortune I have encountered.

I have received immeasurable support throughout my life and I would like to express my sincere gratitude to some very extraordinary people: my late sister Victoria, her best friend and our mother, Dorothea, my backbone and love Penny, my son Tommy, my daughter Christy, my dear friend Nancy, my many doctors, my close friend Monsignor Robitaille, Douglas Musgrave, my teacher Jim Gregory, all my friends with the Toronto Maple Leaf Alumni, my many NHL friends, my many Marlboro friends and the two most influential men in my life, my father Stafford Smythe and my grandfather Conn Smythe.

Thomas Stafford Smythe

Acknowledgments

The co-author would like to thank the following for their inestimable help in the writing of "CENTRE ICE":

- Heidi Winter, who introduced me to this project almost a year ago. Never dreaming that I'd end up being selected as co-author, I extend my heartfelt thanks for your unconditional trust and support.
- C. Jordan Fenn, the publisher and driving force behind "CENTRE ICE," my thanks for choosing me to complete Tom Smythe's dream — in the process, you completed mine.
- Tom Smythe, who inspired me with his story on and off these pages, I thank you for the privilege of sharing your life and treasure the friendship that has evolved.
- Penny Brown, Tom's wife and incredible support, who tolerated visits to her house and calls at home, the cottage and every other sanctuary. I thank you for your patience and hope I make you proud with the Tom I captured on these pages.
- Steve Waxman, Kim Cooke, Ian Marchant and Bruce Barker-four modern guys who listened to my hockey stories through the years and pushed me to follow my journalistic dream. I will never be able to thank you enough.

- Cam Gardiner, my life-long best friend from Windsor, who called me every single day to monitor the progress. To you I give my deepest thanks.
- Andrea Orlick, who works with me at the SONG Corporation, and who used her previous life's experience to guide me in the world of publishing. Thank you for your excitement.
- Tommy Gaston, who sits near me at the Leaf games and regales me with stories about the Mercantile League, Turk Broda and the Toronto Young Rangers. My thanks to you.
- Phillip Pritchard of the resource department at the Hockey Hall of Fame; my thanks for allowing me access to your files, thanks for returning my phone calls even when you were on vacation, and thank you for your generosity and your enthusiasm for my various projects.
- Jack McLean, my cousin and dear friend, who played for the Toronto Maple Leafs during the war years, winning a Stanley Cup in 1944-45. Thank you for all the information you provided.
- Margaret and Gerry England, my mom and stepdad, who made even the craziest of deadlines tolerable with the knowledge that "CENTRE ICE" would make them proud.
- My father, who introduced me to hockey and the Toronto Maple Leafs 40 years ago. I know that no one would have enjoyed "CENTRE ICE" more.
- To my brother Dale, who shared the bowl of chips with me each Saturday while watching Hockey Night in Canada from the time we were toddlers — thanks for your continued love of the game, and even though you now live in Vancouver, I appreciate the fact you still love the Leafs.

Index

C

N

O

P